One Degree South of God

Dynamic Updates on Wisdom and Truth

Volume 1

Transmissions from the Rhammah Masters
Channeled by Jeremy Anacker
Transcribed and Edited by Diane Doughman
Poems compiled by Katherine Grace Sims Kiesch

One Degree South of God

Dynamic Updates on
Wisdom and Truth
Volume 1
by
Jeremy Anacker, Diane Doughman and Katherine Grace Sims Kiesch

Visit our website at www.StillwaterPress.com for more information.

First Stillwater River Publications Edition

ISBN-10: 1-946-30090-X

ISBN-13: 978-1-946-30090-4

1 2 3 4 5 6 7 8 9 10

Cover Design by Jeremy Anacker
Photograph by Orion Kiesch/Happen Media
Channeled by Jeremy Anacker
Transcribed and Edited by Diane Doughman
Poems compiled by Katherine Grace Sims Kiesch

Published by Stillwater River Publications, Pawtucket, RI, USA.

Publisher's Cataloging-In-Publication Data
(Prepared by The Donohue Group, Inc.)

Names: Rhammah Masters, author. | Anacker, Jeremy, medium. | Doughman, Diane, transcriber,
    editor. | Kiesch, Katherine Grace Sims, compiler.
Title: One degree south of God : dynamic updates on wisdom and truth. Volume 1 /
    transmissions from the Rhammah Masters ; channeled by Jeremy Anacker ; transcribed
    and edited by Diane Doughman ; poems compiled by Katherine Grace Sims Kiesch.
Other Titles: Dynamic updates on wisdom and truth
Description: First Stillwater River Publications edition. | Pawtucket, RI, USA : Stillwater River
    Publications, [2019]
Identifiers: ISBN 9780692371367 | ISBN 0692371362
Subjects: LCSH: Spiritualism. | God. | Wisdom--Religious aspects. | Truth--Religious aspects. |
    Self (Philosophy)
Classification: LCC BF1261.2 .R43 2019 | DDC 133.9--dc23

DEDICATED TO ALL OF HUMANITY

Table of Contents

WHY?

AN INTRODUCTION
TO THE DISCOURSES
By Diane Doughman

The wisdom presented here both enhances and goes beyond any other wisdom that is available in today's world. It takes you on a journey deeply into yourself. If you are ready for a new way of imagining the Divine and making better sense of the realm we are living in, then these teachings may appeal to you. This wisdom presents a whole new paradigm for the nature of God. It frames the reason and purpose of human existence with concepts in step with the modern world, spring boarding our imaginations towards possibilities that are both exciting and expansive.

Some of these concepts can be challenging, but this body of knowledge is offered openly, without requirements, demands or expectations. We are given absolute freedom to accept any part, reject any part, or utilize these discourses as we individually choose. They can stand on their own or be used as updates woven into the fabric of a person's other beliefs. The wisdom of the Rhammah Masters takes us further into concepts that our advancing knowledge has prepared us for.

The source of this wisdom comes from a group of masters who operate as a collective consciousness. They present mainly through one voice which they have called Rhammah. We are told, however, that the wisdom is sourced from many masters. Rhammah is channeled through a host personage who is able to leave his body and allow this collective to speak and operate that body. (*See Intro to Channeling for more on this.*) Jeremy Anacker, who channels Rhammah, is a deeply spiritual person of high character, good integrity and profound humility. The ability to do this work is one of a number of gifts and abilities he has.

These transmissions began in 2005 and have been continuous since that time. The discourses have all been delivered to live audiences of quite ordinary people from many backgrounds. Participants present questions beforehand and the Rhammah Masters weave the answers into their dialogues. They also respond to the individual and collective awareness of the persons present with great respect and uncompromising insight. Their answers guide us to an understanding of our greater spiritual nature as infinite and eternal beings.

The title of this book, "One Degree South of God," was chosen for a reason. In the early days, numerous participants wanted to know where these masters came from. The answer we were given was One Degree South of God. This assertion has been slipped into discourses at various intervals since that time. It could have many interpretations. It probably isn't a physical location, for God as Oneness is equally everywhere and in everything. Perhaps it is a state of consciousness or a level of communion. Many students think it means that the perspective these masters bring is extremely close to the most accurate understanding of God possible for humans. You may do your own speculating about this mystery, and there are no wrong answers.

One thing, however, is quite clear. There is an urgent need for wisdom like this. Our current human era has gone global and our knowledge and scientific understanding has accelerated very rapidly. Travel, migration and media have brought cultures together, widely dispersing ideas and belief systems. Doubts and conflicts have arisen as a result of this. The Rhammah Masters have responded to humanity's call for greater understanding. They offer spiritual updates that can better help us bridge our differences, exist in global harmony and cope with new technological challenges.

The most prominent theme of this wisdom is that we are infinite, eternal beings created from a single source of infinite love. As humanity, we are living in a realm of choice where we create our own consequences and learn lessons throughout our many journeys of the soul. We are created from divine love and are never condemned or cast out from that love. The Rhammah masters are kind, compassionate and nonjudgmental. They are not interested in having followers or being worshiped. Many of those who have been studying this wisdom find it helps them make better sense of the world and helps their lives be more balanced, accepting and trusting. It also makes them feel like there is a more expanded and meaningful reason for their existence.

There is great depth to this wisdom. It is best to approach it with an open mind, chapter at a time, and let it settle in. Our human conditioning is tenacious and shifts in perception take time. We are beings with a three-dimensional perspective in a multidimensional matrix of existence. Our limited senses and awareness cannot fully grasp the seeming paradoxes, the vast and complex realms of infinite universes and intricate layers of creation. Throughout human history, spiritual information has been given at levels which humankind could grasp. This is why updates and revisions are periodically needed. And it is time to be invited to the greatest knowing.

You will know if these teachings are right for you. If they are not, go in peace knowing you are loved equally by the Divine Creator. You are free to find your way home in any way and any timeframe you may choose. The Source of our life and being is One. Throughout time it has been named, written about and depicted in many ways, and all ways are accepted and embraced by this loving Source. We live in it, are an intimate part of it and cannot ever be separated from it. If that sounds good to you, then enjoy the journey of these words.

INFORMATION
ABOUT CHANNELING
By Diane Doughman

The phenomenon of channeling has existed in human history since ancient times. It has been a source of wisdom for prophets, oracles, priests, seers and shamans. It is also the likely source for parts of many different religious scriptures. There are a variety of ways in which the process of channeling presents. These can range from enhanced inspiration, automatic writing, meditative trance transmissions and full body channeling.

Basically, channeling allows for information from a non-human source to get relayed through a human. For example, the Koran is claimed to have been transmitted to Muhammad through the Archangel Gabriel. Judaic Old-Testament prophets may have also received spiritual insights, knowledge and predictions in this way. A well-known modern-day channeler was Edgar Cayce. "A Course in Miracles" and the newer "A Course of Love" are both channeled wisdom.

When a person who channels completely leaves their body and the body is inhabited by another spirit being, it is called "Full Body Channeling." In this type of transmission, the human host has no recall of what happened or what was said. This is how the wisdom of the Rhammah Masters is transmitted. The discourses are spoken to live audiences through the body of a man named Jeremy Anacker, who serves in this capacity with great humility, honesty and humor.

Since childhood, Mr. Anacker has had the ability to see and hear energetic beings. He has other psychic gifts like the ability to fully see the human aura and various energy patterns not generally visible to others. For over 27 years Mr. Anacker has practiced Reiki and energy healing. He has engaged in a variety of studies on higher conscious states and advanced wisdom. He is a considerate teacher and healer in his own life.

At live sessions, Rhammah speaks while seated, and the Host's eyes always remain closed. However, at times Rhammah gets up, gracefully walks around the room giving individual blessings and sometimes interacts with physical objects in the room. This is possible with the eyes shut because the masters are operating the physical form from outside of the host's body. They can see everything from that expanded vantage point. This phenomenon is quite remarkable to experience.

Channelers claim or are told that various beings are the source of their information. But no source of channeling, psychic transmission or divination can be verified or proven. People have always accepted the premise of prophecy and spiritual messages on faith and by the worth of the wisdom and their trust of the host. This is equally true of most spiritual things that humans believe. We can't empirically prove that God exists. The existences of angels, spirit guides, demons and ghosts are largely subjective. Spiritual information of any kind should be evaluated on its benefit, its values, its power to uplift and if it resonates with one's heart and spirit.

The Rhammah masters have said: Rhammah comes animating the vessel (*Host's body*) on the behalf of you. Where have I journeyed from? There is the farthest star and there is the universe after that and its farthest star, and that again and again. One world after the other. I come from that great distance in the flows of energy. And as I come, I am with you, setting forth this teaching so that it is known in your body for your benefit. We are eternal, infinite beings of forever, as are you. We are the infinite love of Source which is your true nature as well. It is all one.

BIOGRAPHIES OF THE PRODUCERS

Jeremy Anacker, who channels Rhammah, is a person of high character, great integrity and profound humility. Since childhood, Mr. Anacker has had the ability to see and hear energetic beings. He has other psychic gifts like the ability to fully see the human aura and energy patterns that are not generally visible to others. For over 27 years Mr. Anacker has been an advanced Reiki practitioner and energy healer. He has engaged in a variety of studies on higher consciousness and advanced wisdom. In addition to this he is an artist, is married to a medical researcher and has one child.

Diane Doughman, who transcribes and edits the Rhammah discourses has a degree in creative writing and journalism from the University of Wisconsin-Madison. She has studied the many great world religions, visited numerous sacred sites, and taken teachings with a variety of spiritual masters. She owned a metaphysical bookstore for over ten years where she hosted numerous psychics and mediums. She was married to a successful financial advisor for 47 years. Now retired, she is the mother of three adult children and has six grandchildren.

Katherine Grace Sims Kiesch, who is inspired by the Rhammah discourses, has crafted the poetry that is offered here. She is a graduate of University of Wisconsin-Stout in marketing. She and her late husband Peter (*pharmacist*) have travelled since 1970 seeking out teachers and spiritual experiences. She ran her own business for 18 years. She is the mother of two adult children and grandmother of three. She and her dog divide their time between Wisconsin and Florida.

PART ONE

ALIGNMENT

BE STILL AND KNOW

Get on a ship...... Cross the sea...... Hold steady

The wisest say, "Behold the heaven that you seek, and yearn for it in your

heart. Be still and know"

This phrase is the ship you get on

Put your sail up

Let it take you on a journey

Trust the winds

Hold the rudder in the water

Choose and maintain alignment

Navigate through real realities

Look through the clear lens of spiritual truth

Know yourself as freedom

Be still and know

Discourse 1: Realities on the Journey of Awakening

Rhammah is a being who is also a collective of beings, who is also infinite love itself. Reflect on the fact that the wind blows as an expression of infinite love. There are cosmic winds ushering themselves through galaxies, solar systems and vast fields moving like the wind. Rhammah is all of that and more, and so are you. Rhammah maintains that knowing and we are here to remind you to be with that knowing. Humans are in a myopic state where you cannot see the forest for the trees. This is so because you are willing and also because it is designed to be thus in the human experience. Your strong denial of this makes it enormously difficult to move past what holds you from a breakthrough into higher comprehension. To maintain a desire for such a breakthrough does take help. It also takes power.

Your earthly winds have often been harnessed for energy and for travel. Descriptions of the wind are used by poets for reflection, and on new theories for navigating one's way through life. You might sit on a hilltop and let the wind speak to you through the way it presses you and moves your hair. Similarly, we are the energetic winds that blow through this room. Rhammah presents as a "We," as an "I," and also as an "It."

Maintaining this enigmatic pretense is a service. We show up here with the intention to move past all pretenses, all the conclusions made by this myopic vessel that is termed human. As magnificent as being human is, it is also subject to evolution by your endeavors, by what you yearn for and focus on.

Those who have achieved moments of truth in the arts, in music, in dance have all done so through staying steadfast during the various weather conditions this human vehicle produces. It is not so different from the stories of old where ships could be taken by monstrous waves in the sea. In spite of that, courageous souls would stay steadfast and cross the sea for a vision, for truth, for a potential in humanity be it greedy or virtuous. Somehow it ended up being a part of creation and brought betterment to many lives. All endeavors end up that way because Source, God is everywhere. And Source, God wins eventually, always. It may seem mucked up with the way the media glamorizes and sucks you in and promotes itself. Your media has methods to keep itself relevant. This creates a deep harm, but it is also a mirror. For all of you get sucked into your own pettiness, your own hurts, medicating them with chocolate, possessions, sexuality, with substances, whatever you think works.

So, how much of that are you willing to look at? How much can you barrel through? The shadow parts and the forces of nature in you are not too different than how the seas played upon the sailors in their great ships. Are you willing to be steadfast like them? Who chooses when it is time to move past your crap? And how badly do you want awakening? Are you willing to be grateful to the soul who pressed enormous evil upon you? That would be holding steadfast through a storm with gratitude, in kindness and understanding. Insist on being an understanding, discerning soul, one who learns truth and maintains a boundless life of presence. Empower your life with a true alignment to joy. And inhabit your body and life in such a way that seldom would you become a victim.

At least half of what is termed enlightenment or awakening is facing your crap and moving into mature healing. You must look at the conclusions in your psyche that do not serve you and adjust them. Create specific visions for yourself, whether they are concrete like an increase in income, or whether they are more abstract like the ability to discern in the subtlest ways. The other half of what is termed enlightenment or awakening is to know that it takes the power of grace. Grace supplies the power, the timing, and the circumstances. The field of love is evolving in itself and you are a part of that. Circumstances unfold in such a way that you are chosen, in part because the earnestness is present and in part because you've earned it.

The greatest storm that one would hold steadfast through is the storm to enlightenment. To get in that ship and cross that sea you need to hold steady through the enormous storm that is supplied by the human intellect to understand it. You press forward even as there is karmic fear and lack of pre-knowledge about the land you are moving towards. The sages, saints and masters speak of this place, this territory. The wisest say, "Behold the heaven you seek and yearn for it in your heart. Be still and know." That phrase is the ship you get on. Put up your sails and hang with that phrase and let it take you on the journey. Trust that the winds will take you. Choosing manifests in the form of holding the rudder into the waters and maintaining the alignment. Then you must continue to choose that alignment.

This great endeavor is often undertaken while living a normal life and navigating through very real realities. These realities create an impetus to see circumstances which are unsettling through the clear lens of spiritual truth. Then you know yourself as freedom. You know that all of life is dancing to the will of Source. And ultimately, by the will of Source it moves. It certainly seems as though there is choice and human endeavor at work. And the drama takes you on a trip. Henceforth here you are, in a dance of what seems very real and also what is not. So, be still and behold that which you seek, for heaven is here in your heart. Be still and know this. That pointer frees you from the very real circumstances you are currently in. Hang with it and be still, be still.

Insist on living in an ecstatic space where your sinuses are cleared up of intellectual congestion. Think things over with your friends. Touch your humanity in each choice you make, but desire freedom above all else. In many ways your friends, your helpers, your teachers, your therapists are secular worker bees. They can become guides when you decide your life is spiritual and everything is a product of spiritual realities. When you decide it's all God, you will see the face of your guru everywhere. Are you willing to decide to pursue the way of living we are delivering here? Is it time for you? Call on spiritual reality. Call on it in whatever way works for you. Call on the Lord of your Being, on the spirit within, the pie in the sky, the higher will or the Source of all. Call upon it earnestly. Do you need to hold off using those habits that you escape into? Will you live in such a way that you won't settle for anything else but Source to carry you through another day?

You must realize that all you have earned and purchased through effort can become a cage. In a transforming entity, the construct of function collapses and reforms constantly. What seems true shifts constantly. What is apparently the answer slips through the fingers all of the time. There is always a need for a plan, a need for being able to bob, shift and bow to the moment on every level. If you do not want that, you do not want awakening. The construct you rest your whole soul on could shift. Maturing as a spiritual being you become more resilient to such shifts. You stand on eternal ground instead of the ground of personal passion. You stand on the ground of spiritual fire, living in it and for it. You live the dream of a human, with the fire of one transforming. You give from a space that does not expect return.

Can you give this or that up tomorrow? It's a good question. For what you are seeking is the capacity to allow creation to dance in your personal life. Know that the stickiest areas are those you have invested in the most. Those choices that stabilize you are good, but look into them. Stay with them from a spiritual space. As an eternal being, write your check to the car lot. Function with that vehicle in gratitude. When you live in a spiritual space and you lose what you depend on, you will not hurt. There will be no pain. But, the underbelly of your being is the storm. If you are not facing it and pressing through it with intention, you are not on course.

You may smile and put on a show for your friends. But those areas of your being that produce great storms are where the exhilaration of awakening really happens. Moving into these forces of self does take spiritual help. As you endeavor to go into your own shame, you need to be kind to yourself. And that kind of kindness is a spiritual thing offered by Source, just as it may awesomely be offered by a true friend. Facing these areas of self takes you past judgment. You must live beyond comparison, beyond judging my life to that life. The act of comparing produces the need to have pretense and live in accordance with that pretense. Pretense can be a part of surviving. In many ways it is a part of good function, like presenting yourself in a way that generates positive energy and good relationships. In the human journey such pretense is often necessary. But it creates a competitive energy that interferes with the awakening.

One must be able to move out of the orbit of pretense and get real. In the same way that one can be addicted to the face they present to the world, one can be addicted to anything. Can you stop, be with your crap and your fear and let the Universe dance as it will? If you are capable and ready for this, you may shed a river of tears as you let go, but you will be cleansed. You may have sleepless nights of weaning yourself off living through a social base. But you might be more willing to do this when you realize that in pretense and judgement you are not only creating suffering but you are keeping the suffering in you and others alive. So, call upon spiritual truth to give you the power to move forth into this new arena.

As you are transformed, somehow you are also being more free. Your sense of function will begin to come from intuition. In awakening there is no staying structure. Your being becomes more like a collapsing and reforming matrix. If you want to know how to dance through the maze of needs in this new posture, study a moving mandala and be like one. You will need intuitive help to navigate through the energies of yourself and of others. Each moment can call for a different thing, a different need. There are basic presumptions in the previous human vision that you have given to others and decided upon for yourselves. You will need some dynamic awake space to balance this. For, harmony will only come in those moments when you are willing to be the person you've not yet ever been. Are you up for that task? It is immensely noble.

Indeed, how could there be a higher path than to be willing to put all aside for a dynamic, responsive existence in true reality? That is only possible if the winds of Source are blowing through you, animating and guiding your process. So quite simply, check in with your spirit each moment. Let that practice grow and grow as function, intuition, insight and decision making become easier and easier. The sense that the universe is taking care of itself in you and around you will become more and more palpable. Reality is a seamless expression and there is no defined line between you and others. There is no defined line between what's in you and what is out here. Spirit is behind it all. It is One, a seamless dancing mandala.

If you endeavor to be that, you will be matching up with how reality actually is. You will fall into its excellence and its luster, its high expression and its evolution. You become part of its cutting edge, its crest as it presses forward in you and through you. Your current circumstances are joining up with somebody you haven't been yet. And that somebody has not got it all figured out. That new you doesn't know. But if you stay in that dedicated space, knowingness is immediately available. We are encouraging this land of yours to awaken in its various qualities. There are those in history who lived in one part of this land and were able to travel and speak to larger chunks of it, sometimes the entire whole of it. The awakened way, the enlightenment tells one soul to sit still and be peace. It tells another to give and be charitable. Another is told to teach practices and refine themselves, to be disciplined and be with God through earnestness.

To be a human is to be blind to so many things. But you can choose to be open to an interpretation of life that comes from a different level of reality. Honor that path, that realm of endeavors, for on some level you must know you are being asked to avoid less and face more. This path asks you to be here with spirit, with heart, and to smile more, function more, and take care of yourself. Learn to handle various situations bit by bit as you walk this path. It helps to know where your ship is headed, where the ultimate vision and destiny of all your work culminates. A lifetime is many things, but it sums up in such a way that you become one thing.

A soul can become more independent in a lifetime. It can become more capable, more allowing. That is why the soul comes in and agrees to service, in order to arrive at that end. You are actually being called to be mature, on time, capable, functional, and to say yes to the world and its limits. Awakening has basically two dimensions. There is one where you face your functioning self and handle it on the level that it needs handled on. You grow up.

On the other side, grace is in charge and your sense of choice is useless. On the first side your sense of choice needs to be honed and defined quite completely. Then, that can be used in your posture to be with the grace of Source. On the winds of infinite love, you are taken to new lands.

Do you want that? Are you here for that? What if I say, "That is why you're here and the role you play is superfluous? It's becomes hardly important at all when your destiny is focused on the realization of who in truth you are." What will be presented as you leave this world? As you leave this world you will not wish that you made a bigger buck. You will not wish you had worked more hours. You might say, "I wish I sat with children more and became like them." You might consider saying at the end of your life, "I wish I was more responsive, elastic, alive." That's because the winds that carry you to the heavens ask that of you so you can fly.

It is possible to move into one world and then the other and become like Rhammah, like the wind. And to become like Rhammah is to become what you originally are, infinite love. Affirm this. Sit with it and use it to charge your batteries. For still there is work to be done. And in your loftiest, inner most, highest space it is all good and there is nothing to be done. The part of you that cannot handle that paradox is a great storm that you just might be ready to barrel through. Rhammah bids thee adieu. We are all very impressed by all of you. Until next time, adieu.

THE GIFT

What a great gift, a crack to the ego

It is how the light gets in

Believe it, it is so right

Reality can be like granite

It hits you hard

Every day there are gifts

You are here to serve and help others on their path

How might you involve yourself?

What is the best you can do for the world?

Discourse 2: Living in a School for Angels and Guides

While I see troubles in your energetic fields, I also see the various ways love presents itself, for I am love presenting itself. I am the quality of love that is of the infinite reality which is of forever and is indivisibly inseparable from you. When I say I am a master, I know that I am standing for all the many masters who partake of this wisdom, for we are all of that nature. This reality invites itself to be in you, presenting through you as you inseparably. Even your ego trips, all the games you play as a human are of that masterful reality in some way. The only thing you need to change is knowing that at the helm of that mind-body, at the helm of this life is a master.

This central figure in your dream is the one that you awake to, the organism that you inhabit is the presentation of a master. Look through everything that you are ashamed of, uncomfortable with and troubled about. The best, the worst and all of your parts, look through them to love. See what is really in there when you look in the mirror. When you have a hangover from a month of hiding, look to see what is really in there. Did you know that you can have a hangover from hiding? You can also be hung over from chocolate, from being busy or many other escapes. You have a crash experience and you can't get up for hours because you are hung over from your own melodrama.

You don't realize how hung over you are from being mediocre humans. (*Laughter* You have no idea how much sobering up you can use. The degree to which you choose to discover love, is the degree to which you will discover how much crap you put on others

11

and how much mediocrity you inhabit in a day. But as you discover infinite love, you will love yourself anyway. Say to yourself, "Boy I love this crazy schmuck I've been. I've been willing to be better for years, but boy do I love myself anyway. I am love and I have seen it because I have asked. I have intended to look through all of the murk and the mire and see the god within."

Doing this strengthens you to see clearly in the mirror. But don't look for your shortcomings without an alignment to love, for you will beat the holy crap out of yourself. Put your heart's intention on unconditionally being a master. You may have been lost in various ways which is understandable for you've become humans. You are living human lives with human ideas, instructed in different ways through the years. So, all that presents is both soft and hard, wobbly and stiff, troubled and self-centered. You have a "me focus" within your human perspective, but all of it is right in the "School for Angels," in the earthly school for "Guiding Representatives."

Yes, you are all in school. All of your friends and all of your family, as schmucky as they might be and as schmucky as you might be. All of you are here to learn how to help others on their path. You might be out of body or in your body when you do so. We invite you to engage with that now in all the ways that are made available to you. Do it especially in the most central way, which is to look at yourself with loving eyes. Inhabit your vessel with love and look upon your past as infinite love would look upon it. Find a new way of seeing your human story, one that has a gentle demeanor. Look into the most shadowy moments and bless them. Recall the most shadowy creatures of your past, those who influenced you in negative and mean spirited ways and bless them.

The people that you see in each day, bless all of them both saintly and angry, kind and malicious. Just give loving energy. You can silently say, "From the very Lord of My Being to the very Lord of Your Being I acknowledge divinity. Bless you, I acknowledge the divine in you as well. Bless you, from the Lord of My Being to the Lord of Your Being we are one, unconditionally one. Not a thing that I have ever done or that you have ever done will take that fact away." This fact has gravity. No matter how much harm you place on your brother, he is still your brother. And that is true in reverse. Some brothers have been very schmucky to each other and perhaps they still are. But you can step aside from a competitive nature. It can be gone beyond so that brothers and sisters find each other again.

You all have forms of ego mania that make you unable to hear many things. It is alright. This ego mania can affect various decisions in your day. If you have to make decisions when you've just been injured emotionally, find ways to put yourself aside. Make a clear cut decision based on analysis without allowing the hurt and damage you've just felt to get in the way. A master moves towards making measured decisions, rational decisions after a rational analysis. Each matter is held up to the light of one's own wisdom through the master within. In your conduct, get used to bringing forth the master that is within you. Intend to be the Lord of Your Being in each decision. That decision represents another place on the planet where a higher vibration has taken root. Look for every way you can stand up for a higher vibration. Do it in every little decision in your day.

You can do it in how you pour your milk or coffee. Think to yourself, "As I pour this cup of coffee, may every drop represent all beings of all times and of all worlds. As I sip this cup of coffee, may all beings of all worlds be blessed by this radiant healing power that is of my godly nature, which is in all." With each sip the Universe is lifted. Be a master and find a way so each moment represents truth. Realize that with a kind act or a gesture of love you are representing all beings and the truth within them. As you give a dollar to a homeless person or a meal to one in need think, "As I am friendly to my brother and to my sister, may I be putting another footprint of the higher heavens on this Earth." By doing this you are graduating, for this is a school for future angels and guides. It is school for those who would represent the divine and be helpers even as they are helped.

Unseen masters are all about you right now. They go on like an ocean, one after the other representing infinite love. They represent their own affinity with you and their connection to you, for they are you. They know this and in many ways have been through your troubles. There are also those who graduate but remain in form. They make it to the great heights of reality while in their body. These masters find a way to show another how to stomach the process of movement up the mountain of self. They help them get past the thought patterns, the identities and forces in the quagmire of being a "me" in the clever hall of mirrors.

It is a real challenge to teach for a long period of time, or to start up a religion that will last for two-thousand years. There are specific teachings designed to help those few people who can stomach enlightenment and handle the movement up the ladder. There are also many masters who have not been students of this world. They have come from the heavens and are presented to those here. Their intent has been to turn around the masses, to urge them to move out of a barbaric demeanor and start behaving sisterly and brotherly with love for each other whenever possible. (*A participant asks, "Are they in human form?"*) They have been in human form. You have your Jesus who came directly from heaven as man. He was not a student of this world. It was a great landing. He taught humans to be kind to others and to turn their thinking around.

(*A participant asks, "Was Buddha the same?"*) Buddha was a teacher for the few who can stomach the movement all the way up the mountain of self-enlightenment while in form. Very few can handle it. Both are great gifts to humanity. Humanity will never be the same. One being can lift the whole planet because they are

14

enlightened. Or many beings may act a little bit kinder for all of time. They are both gifts, are they not? And there are so many different ways that wisdom has been presented and is being offered with slight adjustments both small and grand. Divinity and how it presents itself in so many teachers is a complex thing. And the shadow side, which can present itself in some "so called" teachers who had good intentions but fell off the path, is also complex. Some religious leaders have been feverish about their popularity, egoistic over how much they can sell and how big their franchise can be. They can lead others astray.

So, what are you to do with all of this as individuals who want to graduate? Find your little place in the world and get started with this movement. Why not become a better person? There are some of you who are interested in manifesting that in the household. Why not have that and more? Mow the lawn like a master. Think to yourself, "With each step may every atom in the universe feel this lawn mower's vibration as if it was radiating divine love." Find a way to frame every moment while you function. Say, "Today I wake up and I arrive to the tasks of my day on behalf of all those who have felt they can't, those who felt like they don't have enough or are not good enough. Today I am going to be good enough. Today I am going to be happy in spite of gnarly faces and grouchy people. I am going to be happy because I know there is not enough happiness here. I will be that place on the planet where happiness starts running."

When you do a task the divine can amplify it so that with each task the knowing that you are this masterful presence will grow stronger. Being a master is representing the heavens, representing your movement into this sublime truth whatever it takes. So, here you are with a body that you have to take care of. Say to yourself, "Here I eat healthy food. On the behalf of all those who do not have food or can only afford unhealthy food, I put healthy food into this

15

body. May all hungry people be blessed by this experience. I hold them in mind with love and I am experiencing fullness on their behalf. May this fullness manifest itself in a magnified fashion as I own it and deserve it. May all beings be blessed by such an experience."

This is what you deserve in the next movement towards nobility. Desire what you would desire, intend what you would intend after putting yourself out in humility to the Divine. Say, "Guide me, oh sublime force. Infinite Intelligence of the Universe you are of my being. You provide every heartbeat in this body, every movement of blood. Each moment is evidence of infinite intelligence and I choose to be guided by that intelligence. I am humbled by its brilliance. Guide me this day. Guide my choices. Guide me." If your role is to do the most mundane tasks, ask for the insight on how to be more present with them. Ask to see the whole universe in this moment as you wash a dish, as one foot goes in front of the other in your home. Ask to be inspired by truth and to have a truly inspired life.

When you do this you are lifting all worlds. For indeed, as multidimensional beings you have areas of yourself in other worlds. There are so many things that play within you. Ask to be unified and present with this. Think to yourself, "I know that there are infinite worlds and infinite intelligences. There are gods upon gods upon gods and worlds I can graduate into that are aesthetically perfect. They are the most majestic, magnificent gardens where the flowers dance like living mandalas from one color to the other, robustly reaching for the heavens while they already are in heaven."

We tell you that there are heavens, many heavens and even heavens of the heavens. There are so many layers to reality with a capital "R." But this presentation of reality which you are in is no less than all of that. As sweaty as this body can feel, as sticky and uncomfortable as it may seem at times, it is your job to own the highest heaven. It is your job to have a piece of it manifest here through your affection towards something that is here, towards even one thing that is here. And respect all ways to conceive of and create such higher levels of existing.

There are gods who teach without manifesting into the body. There are also divine ones in your history who have taught in obvious ways and religions have been made around them. There are also those who have taught quietly in the caves with a few people, with great humility. They lift the world with that piece of divinity that they would give, that they would present. And you are all such gods with family members and friends whom you can listen to and be with. Just be with them while knowing the highest heaven. As mundane as any moment might seem, it is your job to see the inseparable reality that the highest heaven is here. Each experience has millions of bits of information in it, from sound to touch to smell to sight, to how your body senses. The infinitely complex moves within itself and presents even more complexity.

So, say yes to your complex body, for it is the vehicle of a master who can represent the highest heaven through one act and then another. Things happen to you that you moan and groan about and pass judgment upon. Perhaps instead you might say, "Thank you for this shock to my financial picture. Without it I would not need to look within again and be humbled." There is no greater gift than a crack to the ego. Believe it, for it is so right. It is how the light gets in with a crack to the ego. At times reality can be just like granite.

It hits you hard and shows you where the masters sit. There are gifts indeed, with every day there are gifts. Can you get through a test while representing the highest heaven? Can you know your birthright is a movement through this world and into the next? If you can do this, you will serve others of this world, your friends and family. You will help them in their lives.

When you leave this body, you will have friends from other places in the universe. You will be dancing the tango with beings you never could imagine while you were in form. You will experience them directly and feel so close to them. All of this is so effortless in the next realm and in the many realms and realms. It is all a complex dance so you might discover all of that and move upward into worlds upon worlds and then more worlds. And those highest worlds, those places of profound wisdom have manifested themselves as masters in your realm. They know the truths of higher heavens while being in this body. It is a profound commitment, a profound responsibility. It is not for sissies, and you might participate in that movement. Learn how to involve yourself.

It is time to act like a master. And masters act lovingly in all they do, be it scrubbing the floor with a toothbrush or singing the prettiest song. They may confidently create a large business that takes care of many households through employment. They may give up everything to live in a cabin without electricity in the woods. Masters do so many things, but their one intent is to know themselves as a master and to give out a blessing. They ask, "What is the best I can be for the world?" The answer is, "One should Always be happy." For being a miserable lost student trying to learn what the master is teaching is for sissies. It's for people who don't want to know the heights of euphoric, strident living.

So, do not grovel in student consciousness, dismiss it. Hold your enemies in mind and then hold your heart up to them. If you have a radical alignment to the god of your being, instantly you will be shown your crap. So, love yourself. Love your ego and all the ways it plays. Just be love. On some ultimate level in some ultimate way nothing is wrong. You are dancing an honest dance in wretchedness and in saintliness. Whatever it is, let it be honest. And now, as you turn your attention towards what is truly real, hold your own hand through the process.

When you wonder why you are not more present with your wife or your friends, know it is because you are worried about yourself and not getting your wants. That is normal human stuff, so own it. You might say, "I decided to go out drinking all night rather than be totally present with you today, honey. It's just how I chose my day. I decided to wreck myself with resentment for the last three days rather than face you in a very intimate way. That is how my ego has been presenting itself. I would rather pull on you than give to you. That is how my ego has been. Now that I am honestly awakened to infinite love I see that. It is a bit unsettling because I see the harm. But I know a part of me is turning around. In the divine light I am having an honest moment. I respect myself for turning these areas around and being honest about them."

Deep inside all of you, the child that didn't get enough is still there. Own it, love it and hold it. You are all of divine love and you can handle this frank, blunt journey by seeing a reflection in the pond of your spiritual community. You are allowed to dance in whatever way you continue to dance. There is nothing wrong, nothing wrong. But you can be more honest and more masterful. You can put more heart into the intention of being a blessing. Tell yourself, "I am an infinite being of love and light. I take each breath with great presence and great affection. I am as infinite with this breath as I might be with my child or my first love. I am as present with this breath as I might be with the greatest prize of all time, the love of all humans, the attention of all of infinity. Completely with this breath, may all beings of all time and all dimensions be touched and blessed by the radiant healing power of me owning and being intimate with this breath."

Such a practice will infuse all the little parts of you that can turn around so you can be more here for others. And that means that you will be more here for yourself. Of course you will achieve a greater connection to others if you dance the dance of time with them and hold them close to you. Of course you align with others as it equals opportunity and abundance. It equals creating a network of fellows and energizes that network to own each part in the play. It does this so that a community can manifest which represents the highest heaven. You are a group of masters, so in what small way can you act like one? In what way can you intend like one?

To start, hold those you know up to your heart of hearts. Think, "Bless you my brothers, my sisters and friends. I am an infinite being of infinite love and this love loves you. I dedicate this breath to you. As this heart beats, this love beats for you. I am you. I choose to look through all of your shortcomings, all of the ways your ego presents itself. I choose to see through it to the master and vibrate with what is in you that can effortlessly manifest a whole new dream, a dream that reflects your divinity in a whole new way." Trust creation as it dances in each life. And with each breath intend all of the atoms around you to ignite with infinite love. May the highest heavens present themselves in each atom.

As you breathe greater affection, greater knowledge of what is present, the One Source is indivisibly present with all. The master in you sees through all of your doubts, all of your fears, all of your unworthy stories and the busyness of trying to convince others. It sees through the posturing, the sheepish pulling strategies, the front of the class student playing his game or her game. It sees through all these games to master, the master who in its humility is happy living under a tree, or living in a castle, or living with Romans, Germans and Americans. It is happy with a farmer or a broker, always abiding in the truth of his, her own being."

With this wisdom you can be so happy looking at your crap. Yes, I'm that crap and that and also that. Isn't that a hoot? Look at all the mental games you play out. Recognize the ideas, like I've done it all and then some. I probably could outdo all at the mediocrity game. Watch how nowhere I can go. If you are going to be depressed, do it right like I do it. Do everything just like me. Try to take yourselves this lightly, for you can handle what it takes. It is not for the faint of heart, looking at yourself. But it is easy in the light of knowing. So go for it. Go for it now.

(*A participant has a question. She says, "A child that was born to a friend of mine was born eight weeks early, so it's having a bit of trouble. He's doing okay but his lungs need a bit of help. So I have a toy, would you please bless the toy?"*) Indeed, I will bless it. (*Rhammah handles the toy.*) Every little fuzzy part, we collectively tend to every fuzzy part of this little helper. Here is a divine greeter for a young child. We will put into this little fuzzy animal the great helpers. In the same way that I have been with you, I am with this fuzzy creature and all that it is represents. It is the highest heaven and the great virtues that are potentially to manifest through the struggle of being prematurely born. We see the gifts highlighting a golden path for this child. The struggles of a golden path are laid clear by embracing the struggles of a noble being who would take on such a difficulty. We thank you little being for showing us the way, for showing us our soft spots that we might breathe into them and hold you in mind. Beloved little new born being, bless every stone on your golden path. And every piece of struggle is such a gift to us. We will walk it with you little creature, indeed. (*Rhammah hands the toy to a participant.*) Pass the stuffed animal and continue the blessing as you chant Om. We are with you. We are so impressed with all of you. We see the master in you and your ability to handle all that it takes to move into a truly inspired life. Be a true gift to your fellows and especially to yourselves. Rhammah bids thee adieu.

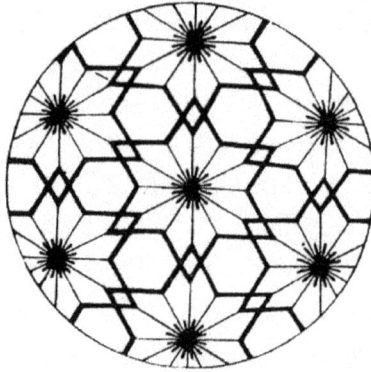

ON A SOUL LEVEL

On a soul level…energies dance like a kaleidoscope of realities

On a soul level…we share layers of our being with others

On a soul level…constant shifts are mixing in you

On a soul level…many realities are being stitched together

On a soul level…we are all entwined energetically

On a soul level…an Interdimensional Matrix…a Universal Transformation

Discourse 3: Interdimensional Matrix of Beings

There are artists who depict the folding of space in optical illusions representative of how this realm is seen by teachers who witness your realm from beyond. Humanity is in a relationship with an interdimensional matrix of castles with many mirrors and many rooms. In this castle one door opens to an area on the other side of the castle where one being lives in a room on the first floor. On a soul level that being is entwined energetically with three others in the castle on three other floors in three other rooms. There are layers of your being like this, ones you share with others that are part of your makeup.

Your individuality is like a cake with layers that are not exactly yours only. These are qualities in the Universe that are evolving. Ingredients, similar to sugar and flour in a cake, are going through a metamorphosis while they are in you. This occurs while they are part of you and are dancing in your makeup. For example, you are sharing realities with friends in this group as it is stitched together. Part of the setup is to have multiple realities dancing at once. Between our visits, there are qualities in you that are shared by others. There is an immediacy and an intimacy that you are not aware of. You are not cognizant that this quality in your own system is a shared quality. To you, it appears to be individual. It appears to be your own thoughts and your own reflections. However, these are set up in you like in any of the others in this group or any group. They are being processed as a group in unity.

There are members on your planet who exist in various places on the planet. They are of an interdimensional matrix that allows them, for the most part, to coexist in the same rooms simultaneously in the great castle. There is an essence to them, an alignment, a resonance. There are others on the planet who are holding a space. And in the interdimensional connectivity they exist in one location. From a fourth dimensional perspective, this collective of beings exists in one location, while they also exist on different areas of the planet holding the energy out of and away from destruction. This handful of abiding, aligned masters exist as one and as apart. You see, the room that they coexist in interdimensionally is a room with a spiral staircase going up, a portal to the next world. It is an elevator that fits alongside a very elaborate setup. It allows one to be on this planet, while also existing in a higher world with this handful of masters that live on this planet, but also live interdimensionally as one.

Indeed, this world is a full range and a challenge to the human mind. Think how all cake has sugar. Like that, all wretchedness contains hate and resentment. It contains the attributes of dilapidated housing. Certain areas of the world that wretched souls gravitate to are of the most barbaric cultures. It is a comfort to such souls to be aligned to the sentiments of darkness, anger and the ease of not evolving. In these alignments you don't have to check your consciousness and move forward. You don't compare your mind with others to see if there is something in you that needs correcting, something like a manipulation, an agenda, pressuring, aggression, pomposity, audacity, grandiosity and so on.

There are so many qualities one can check in oneself by understanding that it is all "your own" mirror. It is evolutionary to crave being with fellows who would mirror back to you. Are you sure you are not letting a "victim like" consciousness take over your day? My brother, are you sure you are not letting an idea "run you" when it is only sometimes true? You have ideas like, "I'm not man enough to take this job. I am too young to apply for this, too old to be seen as valuable." Do such ideas run you? Are they safety zones, conclusions, a way of being, a story you've bit down on, or a place to stay so that the light is not let in?

The truth is you are constantly called to adventures. There is a shifting going on that is interlocked about you and in you with a matrix of complex, magnificent energies dancing like a kaleidoscope of realities. They mix in you with constant shifting, with a new calling all of the time as you stay connected to your fellows. Staying on top of this alive shifting of the matrix is staying on top of a process that makes each day new. It is indeed about sowing, moving forward and being new. Let this "alive" life play out as a confirmation. Say, "I am witnessing an emergence from the power that is, from this place where I am. This place where I am, it is a projector of energy. It animates a whole play, more alive, more convincing than light dancing on a silver screen with surround sound."

You have sensors in various areas of your body. You are a very powerful, sensitive camera and the life that shines forth gives you sensory experience. It gives you what it is like to have a parched palate, an aching back, the pleasure of sight and the quality of a body rising in its breath and falling. For the most part it does this by itself without your deliberate volition. The heart pumps, and there are so many qualities coming together in each moment. You can sit and almost sense the thumping of your blood in your ears and in your body as the heart pumps. Your attention can slip into the many qualities of this dream.

You have the capacity to experience range and depth. You can look upon the night sky in its mystery. One can look into their own aches and pains to witness the mystery. Consider the awesome depths of blackness in what you call space, where holes can suck up galaxies, stars can get pulled into a matrix, into a fourth dimension. You can also witness the light of day, the sun shimmering on the waters, the rustling of the leaves. These are pleasurable sensations of aliveness. The whole of it is convincing you that all of it is real. In order to slip loose of this hypnotic trance, you need to love the great power of illusion.

Do you know what projects and animates this great dance? It is in you great masters. Inside of you is this quality that stories are written about. Inside of you there are gods projecting and animating through you. The Mayan Gods are a magnificent, mighty, convincing, propelling illusion, as are others. And you amplify the love on this planet for the full range of life, the great horrors and the great joys. It is you turning up that love, saying yes, as if you could reach into the fabric of this illusion and hold it in your hands. Turn up the love of it, and sit with it like it is your own innocent newborn child. You've learned love through the tribulations and joys of your children. Such an experience contains the full range.

Can you back up with Rhammah to this place where there is a yes humming across all of creation? Creation is animated by a force inside of you projecting out. It starts with your own organism, for when the body drops, so does the whole dream. They are one, body and dream, and when your body drops, this dream drops not a second sooner or a second later. Your human experience is a great, deeply hypnotic matrix. But don't be overly enamored with it, for it drops. This is very transformative to know. It clings not a second longer. The level of Oneness with the All at work is that intimate, for all of this, whatever is behind it animating your brothers and your sisters is in you as well.

Indeed, this realm is a magnificent spectacle of opportunity. And there are similar representations of these realities which one can graduate into. Also, other worlds, higher worlds can touch down here in this world. And, you can choose to live in the parameters of those higher world's here. Essentially, you can graduate from this world while you are here. There are pockets of opportunities on this planet to sit with those greater worlds. Endeavors like writing, painting, creating, sewing, that is indeed a pocket where those worlds you aspire to are available. Right alongside the most awful things you can be creative and enjoy this entire world without pause, without dissipation. For when it falls apart, the sense falls apart that there is something next in a third dimensional, linear reference. And there is no next in the disappearance into creative energy. In awakening to the greater world, there is no next, no sense that there is anything wrong. Nothing else needs to be done than what is being done naturally.

You see, there are worlds where things are more immediate, where the thought and the dream are more gelled together and you can create your whole world instantly. In that reference, the projector and the world are one. What is taken out in that scenario is the individuated identity because it is fixated. In the expanded perception, the sense of command over the elements comes from the Oneness of it all, not from the character in the dream. There are also worlds where it is just vibration, just power. This power is behind the scenes, driving forth infinite worlds. Analogous to the power plant of your world, it is a type of generator where there is only power and only Oneness.

That Oneness sits with itself and just generates great power, the power of infinite worlds. To the human, such a Creator Force might seem boring and has until now been largely incomprehensible in human comprehension. Thus the play. For if you are bored, we will create stories. If power is not enough, if abiding, magnificent, soft, yet infinitely powerful and exquisitely alive condensed power is not enough, then there are dreams and worlds to play in. And it is all completely right, completely okay. And while that is so true, we would put a fire under your seat. As a friend we would tell you that while there is not a right way, there is a timing to head steadfast to knowing this highest world. Sit in it, and know that from this singular, infinite, always ongoing power, a world is dancing.

On a vacation one finds perspective and humor. It is possible for things to be easy. Why not have this journey be like that. However, while it is possible for one to sit easily in this greater truth, sometimes one needs to be knocked on their ass to get it. Sometimes one needs immense pain to be shown appreciation for higher perspective through that hard line way. For when there is that vulnerability, when you are knocked down, the masters are there holding you in their hands and in their minds. They are showing you an alignment with humility that can only be found when you are deconstructed in such a way that you have no strength. It is like you are moving further sometimes when you think you aren't moving at all. You are being taken to a very real place, a next level that can be experienced only by the nature of what is behind the human play.

The psyche has a hard time knowing how to trust. It struggles to get a sense of what is at work in a realm far greater than anything your mind can conceive. So it must rely on a great trust that great wisdom can come on a day in delight and easy listening. It can also be an ideal time to take in wisdom when you are knocked down. You can allow that you are being adjusted by the loving power of your own nature. Rhammah is within that nature. This Host is inside of you. It is a projection from the power within you. Tell the Host, after you have some discussions, that he is to allow Novo Rhammah in to give all here an energy hit, an energy wave. School is in session, sit. Chant Om. Rhammah bids thee adieu. (*Group oms*) (*Novo Rhammah is another expression of the Rhammah Master group which occasionally presents in channel. One of the Host's gifts is that he is able to go in and out of the channeled state rather easily, which facilitates the type of succession suggested by Rhammah.*)

(*After a group discussion Novo Rhammah comes in.*) There is this Allness. There is also that focus on being what you call individual. What apparently appears as individual is really a part of a great multiplicity. It dances in many ways, interdimensionally and in the

28

physical. There are worlds, a multiplicity animated by the One, by the All. To sit with this wisdom is to sit with a way of being that the human mind can't entirely fathom, that Allness with its absolute power of everything dances simultaneously in such multiplicity.

You see this hand. This is the hand of Allness, the One Power with its multiplicity. Put aside what separates Allness and multiplicity in your minds. Allness and multiplicity, it is one power that is simultaneously many. So, take out concepts which cause you to separate the Oneness of Creator from its created multiplicity. Power and multiplicity are dancing magnificently in you. We take that which separates and put it aside. It is given up. It is the time to enjoy the texture of intellect knowing it gives no answers. Enjoy the "well said" concepts that are useful. These two truths are One, and we take out that which sees two. Make two fists and put them on your knees. Hold all of creation in your fists and be the One Power. Energize it with the foundation of what you are. Hold it and shake it. Shake your fists like this. Shake them like you are shaking a cage. Shake the world you live in and shake yourself. Shake everything and put all of the multiplicity which is Oneness in the middle of your consciousness. It is done. Novo bids thee adieu.

SMILE

Check in with your body…

Smile into the pinches in your energy self

Smile into the tightness…the restriction…the contracted

Smile into the areas that are hard like steel…cold like ice

Smile into the areas that are selfish…tense…agitated

Check in with your body…in with your energy self

Sit often…track it

Now can you smile into the core of it all and unhook everything?

Discourse 4: Universal Life of Allness

It is valid to consider that the full knowing of infinite love is now touching this form. The Host has allowed for a presentation of infinite love expressed as Rhammah. I am infinite love, here as a representative of your greatest truth, for you are also infinite love. On another occasion, in another universe the lesson would now be over. Resonating with that one statement is all the meeting would consist of. We would visit and there would be knowing of infinite love magnified amongst the members of the fellowship. What we do is no different than what you would do with a child, encouraging it into its next stage of development. You also have other beings here with you, one after the other after the other. Each of them fully knows what Rhammah has expressed, that they are this infinite love and it is forever.

Ultimately, if you learn what Rhammah teaches, then all of your questions will disappear in the pool of knowing that is infinite love. They would be answered by it and taken into a new context. Or the questions and answers would fall apart. Your questions arise from a world that is only true like a dream is true. It is not the whole reality, so Rhammah pops open and shines a light on the barriers between this reality and the next. The edge of this reality is not as real as you think it is. Are you aware that you have friends who visit you, ones on the other side and some on this side. When they think of you, you are affected. Tuning in to them is a psychic capacity of life. But we would rather take you to the beloved fact that Allness is one mind. Humanity is one mind, one complex, massive computer-like construct that functions in very complex ways within a body of energy. And within that are contexts of lower and higher forces in each individual that operate as a shared struggle.

In many ways this complex manifestation is one energy, for massive numbers of humans are dealing with the one force that is addiction, the one that is anger, resentment, blame, shame, victimhood, mediocrity and the like. It is one reality, one temptation that is shared by humanity and is not uniquely yours alone. These forces are working on the whole planet. But to help offset those issues, there are beings who are waking up. They do that by moving out of the crap and into these more noble fields of influence. They have a greater cause in humanity by being closer to their true selves and discovering its power and subtlety.

You all have this "Lord of Your Being" that is teaching you in exactly the way you need. For there are different lessons within the massive being of humanity and in the various aspects of energy. Each individual has its unique expressions, its unique signature and the flow of wealth or want. An easy lifestyle or a troubled one is not easily defined. But understand that each entity's higher nature is choosing a life that fits a much needed lesson. It may be about great wealth within a family. Or it could be about pulling together wealth that strengthens your tribe when resources are scarce. Discovering abundance under very difficult situations is often chosen by the entire nature in one's being.

Know that your journey towards changing conditioning often takes the form of moving one's self out of financial struggle, or moving out of lower forces. Perhaps your family was a victim of these and was being taken care of by others in many ways. You saw the pattern and took responsibility for your life, aligning to a more noble or abundant reality. Often in taking such a path the individual struggles. Parts of its being clings to that world it came from even though most of that person has moved into a more abundant, self-responsible life. That one may choose a virtuous life where they have broken the mold, but some last piece of them does not move into the new dream they have created. That last piece is often judgment. It can take the form of resenting the parents who raised them, of resenting their poverty, or of resenting poverty in general within humanity.

Perhaps those who shaped you were selfish and your fight with that creates a sticky spot in you. That stickiness can keep you bound to the former vibrations that you've worked so hard to move out of. An awesome acceptance is needed for those last bits of yourselves to move into the light. It is an acceptance that reflects the very source of your being that is infinite love. That infinite love embraces the most awesome tyrant. It is you knowing that the most awesome tyrant is essentially made of "God Stuff." It may be a twisted form of "God Stuff," an ignorant or misaligned form of it. But there is great virtue in sitting with the fact that such beings are of God, and are also a part of you. You are not to get rid of anything. You are not to push away anything in order for the full movement of grace to take you into a universe of abundance. What is a universe of abundance? It is a state of consciousness immediately available upon the recognition of truth. It often manifests as material flow or a financial breakthrough. However, that is not the whole picture.

You are here in humanity, in a reality of limitations where one thing is possible and another thing is not. There are limitations that keep this game going. It is no different than the boundaries or rules of a board game. So indeed, whatever limitations show up in your life, whatever barriers you feel are there, see if you can go to yourself and smile into your body. Smile into the pinches in your energy self, the tightness and the restriction. Can you go in and unhook even the most heavily configured body of rules and set of principles? Unhook them by smiling into your body, for your body represents everything. It represents all of the many worlds. It also reflects the many dimensions behind this organic presentation that is life with all its forms and adventures. All is available just by being with one's body and sitting with its energy.

So, sit often and track your body. Smile into the areas that are hard like steel, cold like ice, chilly, heavy, disturbing, creepy and horrific. Just be with the Allness, with the multitudes of what you are and smile into them. This smile comes from the Lord of Your Being. And doing this does not mean you get lost in lower forces. It means you are looking honestly at the environment which allows them to take over and run the show. We are referring to the human tendencies to be selfish, heavily configured, tense, agitated, pushy and manipulative. The great infinite space that is the Lord of Your Being looks upon these temptations and helps you nip them all in the bud. We are giving you a way to serve self and humanity. You are sitting in a perfect place to discover the many worlds. So, check in with your body and its energy field. It is the access point of all reality sitting right here. Can you smile into the core of it all and unhook everything?

In this wisdom, we look into all of it. We get down to business and smile into the aggravation and the agitation. You get to contact the place where it comes from, so look into your own body and experience its energy. Know that there are many worlds connected to the one vibration that is you. All universes, all beings are connected to you as you sit here. Intend to smile into the core of this body, into this moment and into the core of all worlds. When you smile into all this and bless it, the world is different for you. You begin to look at where everything flowers from all creation. A personal drama may create the impetus to process one's conditioning from this perspective. You can look under all of it and smile into the core of the universe with complete acknowledgment that the Lord of Your Being is there. Every game that runs its course in you is some type of mental perception. It may be attractive because it is familiar and it seems to work. We are encouraging you to get at that view's very beginning and smile into the place it was created from.

The view that you are broken and need fixing runs from a sense of incompletion or poverty of spirit. But the wealth that is the Lord of Your Being is always available. And do not misconstrue wealth as financial worth. Your state of completion may foster a breakthrough in financial perception. But the Lord of Your Being can say, "All is well when there is nothing or all is just as well when there is plenty." That is the place you are here to discover. As it emanates you can be the silent teacher. But do not ignore that it is possible to share strength with others. You may say, "In many ways I have been in your shoes. I also have a mind that tends to blame external circumstances for my feelings. I am working on unhooking that." You may tell others about the mechanics for understanding human patterns and that the process of blaming is empty. It has no fuel without the recognition of spiritual energy. People can discover this and be able to benefit from it.

So what are these games about? You discover spiritual energy, look inward and sober up to the fact that you are manipulative, that your niceness is a strategy to pull on other people's energy. Why would you want to discover that? It's because you've felt the peacefulness of going home to a place where there are no games. That place is the Lord of Your Being at your very core. There are many human strategies played by imitation. One version is, I am like this and therefore I am special and get special treatment. One may say, it is completely fine to be sick and taken about in a wheelchair or think it is a great service to say yes to the accommodations and kindness of others. Those situations are properly available to those who have very real limitations. But this work is about growing out of the need to pull, the need to feel complete in the game, the need to list versions of "I can't." To say, "I can't climb stairs" is to say when push comes to shove you are not willing to crawl if necessary.

35

Awakening to all these great concepts is heady stuff. But what can happen in this work is that some aspirants discover how important they are to their community because they have experienced their own energetic reality. They also discover their own fear of growth and of being alone. Then they discover the need for attention which is a result of the non-discovery of the Lord of Your Being. Perhaps they create an affirmation like, "I smile into myself. I am ready. I am strong enough to face the games that run. I hereby courageously endeavor to discover the silly games of a human and move through them. I ennoble this being to behave and to become one who participates fully and lifts others." This sounds impressive to those whom the individual wishes to impress. But it can be a total front, a dramatic show.

There are many worlds and places where there are groups of people like this. Each participant somehow brings it, but there is no getting it. The gods in that circle create a magnification and a sense of timing, of music. Are you going to be there to chime in and count the measures? Will you feel the tone of their song so that you can play righteously? How much do you want to hold the energy close, to be present with it? You buy into the belief that to be near the energy is to be closer to the universe, to its love, its genius and its perfect timing. Being in such a state is wonderful. The energy hooks you and you get a little high from it. It doesn't have side effects like drugs might. But it can set you up to play games, to put a toe in the water and just be there for an energy hit. And that is completely okay for that is how it begins. But that can become a way of playing more games. Each human in such groups pretends they haven't discovered it yet and want to know more about it. This game can go on and on.

So, you need to smile into yourself and set the compass for home. That journey is not always pretty. Hold yourself in love and go on that journey. But first have compassion for yourself. Be ready to breathe and be gentle with your games. For you are given encouragement by many of the attributes offered in spiritual communities, to dabble, to prance along and get high off of energy. You get to share in being part of a movement in your culture that is advancing alternative healing and spirituality. In so many ways that is right to do and it is useful to have some assistance. Having some ways of reflecting on the very tough spots assists a person in spiritual growth. But remember that one of the most difficult things that comes up early in one's evolution toward higher consciousness is the very limited level of enthusiasm for growing past ego. It seems like everyone around you doesn't want to grow or even see beyond ego. And somehow one gets caught up in that, in spite of one's desire to transform.

It may be the case that the excitement and support for awakening isn't there in your spiritual community. You are taught to endeavor to create the environment, make the space conducive for encouraging others, or to develop the business. And in spite of that wonderful vision, there are pitfalls because there comes a time when every act needs to be a reflection. It needs to be prayerful and have absolutely no sense of outcome in it. It is an offering to the Universe. Action and creation do need to be balanced with the alignment that you will leave this world alone. The people you touch will not follow you to your deathbed. They will come and go. And some things don't work out because it is necessary that they don't work. Or you may get the breakthrough your ego wants and then it won't move out of its phony position.

The God of Your Being is too big for being phony. It's too real and too humble. It is not enough to be a popular spiritual teacher. It can actually be an impoverishment if you have not discovered truth in yourself in the most real way. And the trials of assisting community can mute your quest. You need to see that each circumstance is an assistance to the soul, rather than seeing every failure as needing transformation into success. Rhammah dares you to see every failure and success as a teaching directly pointing you to the discovery of the Lord of Your Being. Embracing and accepting both failure and success as lessons evens them. This lays at the heart of all experience. Staying very close to it unhooks you from the mental paradox of fame and being forgotten. It unhooks you from being lost, from running games based on conditioned perceptions.

So smile into yourselves. All of you are loved, and you are love. That is where this ship is going. You will be acknowledging the limited forces in your being with gentleness, strength, and a dismissive conviction. Who you really are is a very gentle and lordly way of being, often quiet and when necessary blunt. It is very straight and very even. Before you discovered this world of awakening, all you had was the acceptance of the status quo. And now you have decided to move beyond it, to look past it and discover what is out there. In that process the ego can hook into a place that says, "I am special now. Now I am so special." In order for this conclusion of ego to be countered, one must acquire an aligned acceptance of the status quo. And to serve any discovery of what is beyond the status quo, there needs to be an evenness, a sense of balance with it. Without the status quo, society would not have cohesiveness or the capacity to function. For the status quo is where people feel safe, and you are attempting to test the status quo. So, commit to serving whatever breakthroughs occur in your environment, in your family, your yoga class or whatever situation you are in.

So as you are waking up, there are different elements needed along the way. You might prematurely dismiss certain wisdoms from your old life that may be helpful in your quest. Those elements are often involved with the daily grind. And there is a stitching of the status quo, because it runs negative to your attempt to be even with the world and how it is presenting itself. Your even vision helps you hold the whole world as a beloved child. It allows you to care about it in such a way that you would give vibration and nurture to whoever in your world enters the discovery that you have arrived to. So, how do you manage these counter forces? It is useful to see this like any dream or moment in your day. In order to find truth, you need to be discerning. You need to be okay with the way consciousness is slippery and moves and changes like the weather. You can acknowledge the dance of one energy and what it's about when it's tuned up. And the capacity to address an un-tuned instrument comes from the intuition we want from you.

It's not easy to be asked to look at yourself. Rhammah presents a style of consciousness, of abiding that is quite freeing. It's surprisingly easy when it is time for you to apply it. There will be points of release on your journey in the years ahead as you delve deeper into this world of healing and spirituality. At some moments you may feel like you have arrived. At other times you may feel like you are starting over. And there are things being activated that can be heavy and troublesome. So be appropriate with yourself. Often you need to get on the table and get a healing, or be taken care of by others and be vulnerable. The true sign of an advanced aspirant in this work is one who allows others to help them. Can you turn yourself over and open up, even to a beginner or to someone who is brand new?

In this teaching we encourage a sense of positivity. But is this path about being a positive person? Initially perhaps yes, but that can set up a judgment with one's self. That thought-form becomes a war with this judgement, if one is negative they are no longer on track. But you are all very real and Rhammah loves all aspects of you. So the space we invite you into, and the space we offer is one where you discover how to give yourself that kind of room. It allows you to dance with yourself in a real way where you are not pretending. You don't approve only of positivity. You are picking up an invitation to reflect, to be with yourself and question what presents itself as complexity and the dynamics of many points of view.

We are asking you to look into a place that is way beyond positive. Your authentic self tends to be revealed as creative, harmonizing and dynamic. Beyond judgment it is a way of relating to everything that seems to work very well. It will have traction and function with power and lack of effort. You are all doing so well. Rhammah bids thee adieu.

GARDENING

Compost

Rich fertilizer

Diverse soil

Till up the shadow side of yourself

Turn it, look into it, embrace it

Plant seeds

Find your roots

Stretch for the light

Seek a new authentic self

Discourse 5: Embracing Your Shadow Self

We have taken the Host out and set him down in Mother Nature. And we are speaking to him via the birds, breezes and the river as training for listening. We encourage listening in daily life. You might spend time listening to the wind as you let the breeze run over you. Let your body take in all experiences with your whole being, listening to the unspeakable glory that is present. Inexpressible, in-effable joy is available. It becomes palpable and direct as you be-come earnest about sensing it. Practice having more affection for the delights of just being alive and become grateful for life.

So, while the Host is in the woods, we would like you to know that the energy which is given by the unseen masters and given by Rhammah is like the energy of nature. In the mossy moist areas of the forest many creatures and complex interdependent systems are able to flourish. A similar level of complexity is available to humans on this planet. When you pay homage to it in yourself, you are work-ing on it in yourselves. You seek to find abiding truth, and such truth is completely alive in you for its own sake. It is that which has no argument. To seek a noble life is a grand quest. Find focus in that and be discerning about what to disregard. Ask yourselves, "What is the life I choose to live?"

Many humans choose time with their children, with family or friends in balance with honest time spent with themselves. But you all, to one degree or another, lose yourselves in the chaotic forces of humanity and the chaotic forces in your own nature. To balance this, embrace the complexity of your nature as you contemplate truth. Also, embrace all the layers of your nature just as you would embrace all of the forest. For the consciousness that you inhabit does not have a concrete end or boundary. It is a bit like the forest edge which can be defined as a breakdown of the trees, or the beginning of the grasses. But, it is not always clear exactly where that boundary is. Like that, it is not always clear where one aspect of your life ends and where it blends into the next area. So, tonight's lesson is about looking at nature itself and seeing parallels.

To do this, you need to contemplate your own patterns. You will find rich arenas for discovery and areas set up for the continuation of the dark or shadow areas of your being. They are like forest areas with grubs and worms, where a deeper process hides. Ponder whether that is just depth, or if those parts are hiding from the light? Look for ways that the trees, birds, critters and plants are directly benefitted as they live their life in the light of day, but also know they rely on the shadow part of the forest. Be aware of those connections and contemplate how those shadow areas of your being are connected to the rest. Those places where you struggle in your relationships, struggle to finding a way to live authentically, know they are a part of and benefit your whole being.

It is possible for all of your being to exist and thrive in the light and as the light. But all of humanity contemplates the deep places where they hide their actions. Having shadow diversions comes from a drive to establish a uniqueness, a privacy, a special world huddled away where it cannot be touched by others. Too often those parts are huddled away in shame, guilt and apathy. If those areas of self are contemplated, they can be discovered as simply aspects of your totality. Then know that it is really a difficult dance to be a human trying to live an authentic life. One has to somehow acquire the inspiration and motivation to live an affirmative existence, to have community, and to find your charitable nature. Each of you struggles to exist meaningfully with the right commitment, strength and balance.

The effort to do this often gets molded into a motivation to become competitive. Human concepts and conditioning encourages the kinds of accomplishments that push you toward the "me versus them" mentality. You are enticed to obtain and maintain a "better than" status. So, in this discourse, we will incubate in these shadows of the forest befriending the moss, the grubs and the decaying trees. The cool rocks on the forest floor, the decomposing soil, the bugs and worms will be our comrades. We are going to become a part of that world with a gentle eye and an allowing sensibility. You do this metaphorically as an exercise to be alright with your own shadow areas.

Let your guide be the shame, the bashfulness and timidity you feel. Look at your propensity to hide in the spirit of privacy, shutting others out and avoiding community. You all have such aspects and I want you to shine a light into those areas of your being. Give thanks to all aspects of life that thrive on the light and benefit from the shadow. Allow yourself to embrace this moment of experimentation with your privacy, shame, guilt and apathy. Say, "I give thanks to the whole of life which has created the opportunity for me to stew in my own brew and to resist beneficial change." For you are allowed to do so. You are also allowed to experiment with that in many ways and often for great lengths of time. Although it may be trite to say you need to experience the bad to appreciate the good, it is accurate in so many ways.

So, bring love to your being and find an honest conversation with this area of yourself. In order for it to exist at all there has to be delusion. It exists in the greater set of delusions that keep this human house of cards, this very precarious set of stories strung together. For life in its dance is a set of stories and every cell is a story in its own right, every atom, every pulse of energy as well. All aspects of the forest are a unique story. And these stories compile into the multitudes of stories which make up the story of all universes. When you bring them all together, they are the story of the Inseparable One. In this metaphor, you have the richness of potential linked with decaying matter. But notice that the flower coming from the muck can be so beautiful in its purity as it reaches towards the sky.

Authentic transformation comes from your capacity to go into this teaching. Can you track your own shadow into the richness of new potentials for your life? It is not unlike the evolving of various areas of your planet where life has been experimenting, where diversity has emerged. So, we come to remind you of your greatest nature and how it might relate with your current physicality and personality. We do this in the hope that your values might be adjusted. Let a true, staying new alignment be part of your dream, for there is great potential in facing your shadow. In the shadows are the parts of you that contract the most, that you protect the most and that are tucked away the farthest. Gently nudge them towards the warm embrace of the One which includes all beings, all behaviors, all actions and all thoughts. That great One is all that has ever manifested in all of humanity, in all of time, in all beings.

Try to fathom that in the vast expanse of Oneness this world can be understood and seen as an experiment. It is also an experience of shadow consequences and a sense of being lost. For the shadow side pulls one from the higher intentions that life should really be about. In its darkness, this world can be a morbid, confusing place, a virtual hell. The mentality of the shadow side constricts. It makes one experience themselves as more and more distant from others. It is also the thinking that fixates on your egoic concepts of me and mine. So, why not look at your shadow without judgment and understand that it is a common trait of all humans. Even the saintly have had to look at this honestly and become sobered by it. Many times, humans hold themselves above other members of humanity because of all of the wretchedness that has been done. But how can you justify holding yourself above them when such traits also live within you? It is only a matter of degree and circumstance.

This is important, but don't let it overwhelm you. If you were to contact your own nature in its entirety, including your own shadow, you would be stunned by the excellence of your soul's journey, by its honest quest to find a beautiful truth. Focus our words to quicken that knowing. Become aware of how shame and obsessions played out in darkness create worlds. Let the un-faced things emerge as subtle contributions to the collective shadow like an unprocessed, dishonest day of grumpiness. Don't try to get rid of the full richness within the complexity of all of life. Because the full range exists in Mother Nature and also in your nature. So, how dare you go against all of that by going against the grain of your whole being.

It is part of your awakening to pick up this gentle imperative to track your own self. Take all that you are and track it back. This imperative gives birth to an awareness, an authentic process. It is like finding out that you have a nice bag of compost, a rich fertilizer or a diverse pile of mud. You can till the shadow part up, turn it over, look into it and embrace it. For without doing so, new seeds cannot be planted. Unless you address this, the true you will not find the roots. It will not find a new light or an authentic new alignment.

In your human life, there are those alignments that truly matter. Playing with your child and actively helping them learn is about life. Taking time to enjoy something with your partner is about life. Asking yourself to become more physically fit just so you get accepted by others is not about life. Neither is obtaining material goods just to impress others. Joining others in games, dances and bringing your free, empowered self to others is living. That is getting it. Finding an alignment that matters, that is the quest to be contemplated, the ground zero of shadow. So, be aware of how your patterns and behaviors affect your life. That is the rock bottom that you wish to establish.

46

One thing that this means, is to never put yourself above any perpetrator or any culprit in history or in your existence. Such humility is an example of one who is seeing the various subtleties in their own being in an honest way. You don't have to be a serial killer to get over selfishness. Simply realize that the killer has selfishness and so do you. Then say, "Today I will be generous. Today I will smile when the ego says I do not want to. Today I will give items in my home away, even when my ego does not want to." For, there is some relief in letting go of a few items. And there is plenty of relief in letting go of many items that cannot be used. This of course is metaphoric. The alignment you are looking for isn't really about giving stuff away. It's about living undistracted, clear and resolved. It is like the flower coming up straight then bending to find the light as it pulls the moisture through its roots, through that shadow rich soil.

In an awakened being there is gratitude for all of life. There is a deep sense of acceptance for everybody and every part of everybody. Achieving that level involves respecting yourself as an embodiment of Oneness. If you respect the body, for example, you put in materials it can use not things that are empty and toxic. It is similar for the mind, be mindful what you put there too. Affirming your divine nature upgrades the body. So, be gentle with your life, for this planet has a range of choices. The parameters that you live in ask for a sense of striving and a sense of naturalness, a sense of acceptance of self and circumstances. Contemplate that. For living authentically does not mean denial and starving of the senses. It means joining, getting on the floor with your cat, with your pet, with your child and dancing.

Of course, you can hide in a weekend of eating cupcakes. And you can hide through all kinds of subtleties of the ego. You can hide in shame, for humanity offends in so many ways. The shadow of shame arises when you or others value you as better than or less than what is in a multitude of expressions. In the attitude of humility there is gratitude and acceptance for the many who are like you. In that posture compassion prompts you to hold your hand out to somebody who has your troubles. Hold out your hand in a no-nonsense vision of the many reasons one may get lost in the shadows. It happens because contraction is comfortable. It can support those who would nurse a grudge. It entices those who would stay seething in anger and caught by memories of the distant past.

Such uses should not be called wrong or be denigrated. Rather, work with such impulses. For humans can utilize the dark spaces in so many ways. Indeed, if embracing the shadow side is not a part of your full assessment of self, then one's true life cannot be discovered. So, in an honest assessment, choose from aliveness, from natural power, from alignment to truth and letting the greater light be a part of your existence. But don't deny the shadow aspects. The full embodiment of a life includes acceptance of its full richness. This teaching is not meant to justify those who want permission to juice up their ego or to bite down on shadow behaviors with a vengeance. Use this teaching for looking at that energy which is asking for validation. The biggest divine challenge is a teaching that asks you to be of your true heart.

There are parts of your nature that will spin anything to avoid a good challenge, to avoid a process that might create some sense of movement. Driving them deeper into the shadows is contributing to a cycle of stuck energy. It becomes totally stuck and that non-movement is death. It is death of the organism and death of possibility. It hides in a person who has a strong list of rights and wrongs, a strong sense of the correct way to be. This closes a person down and they experience disharmony with others, ostracism and struggle. They find a way to perpetuate the story of victim. If such individuals do not see how they create this from the shadows within, they will stay stuck.

In this cycle, people persist in stuck relationships not wanting to be challenged. They may go from job to job, place to place, name to name and behavior to behavior. For some it can be as bad as going homeless. For there are no friends in that to create a bargain with, none who will turn them around and get them moving forwards. For some, that is what is necessary. And you must accept that you are not better than these others who are stuck. In this teaching, you must see yourselves as equal to all others and that instantaneously corrects your thinking if you stray from that pattern.

Correcting yourself doesn't look like following a set of dictated rules. It is you sitting with the incubation of truth, creating a sense of reflection that births a true sense of choice. Look at how you have done things in the past and how you currently do things. It is obvious there are details that hold you back, things you would not share with others. But you cannot hide from us or yourself. There are no secrets here, but also no unforgivable behavior. Discern the freeing that assurance gives you. Know that being unstuck is living fully. So, strive to be in the light of endless love that Rhammah is. We see all humanity as love. And as we see all the various parts of you in that love, see yourself that way.

Staying stuck in a self-inflicted state of hell is an unnecessary sentence. We aren't asking you to speak up and announce publicly all the crap in your past. We aren't suggesting that you tell the dirty secrets that haunt you. There are professionals who can be helpful in those matters if you need them. But symbolically all of you can clean house. Energetically reach in to the clickity-clank in your energy, those edgy, heavy iron like parts. Dig up those matters in your being that are like rocks. Pull them out and dump them on the floor. Pile them up. Just imagine letting these parts be known by all of humanity. In that symbolic gesture, you will give yourself to humanity and to a true, inspiring alignment. You are giving up what doesn't work to make way for what will work. So, pick a nice juicy trait. Get your hands around the squishy parts that have been in the swamp. Pull them out and offer them to the All That Is.

There is nothing that any of you have done that has not been done by multitudes of people in many ways. So, you are simply joining up with humanity and getting out of the games that your ego plays. Your ego is always racing for high ground, striving for an unchallenged life. It tries to act out the part of a saint instead of being honest and level with its self. Lead the ego to the truth that you are part of All Oneness, part of its exploration with itself. Reach for this model and transform that heavy rock of suffering you unearthed. Find another heavy rock. All of it is forgivable. Take it out of your being and offer it to the All. Say to yourself, "I am forgivable." Say to your own being, "I am a part of the experiment of humanity and that potential is so much grander than my failing." You have no idea how stuck you are until you dump it out.

You can also imagine a great fire where you can dump that which you don't even know you have. Jettison the aching and the sense of suffering that you don't even know you have. For you all have scary, wild shadow creatures in your body, in your energy field. Grab one and let it writhe in your hands before you throw it into the fire of truth. Release the lower world intelligences into the fire of forgiveness. Take away the weight and lighten up. It is forgivable because it is all part of the design. Be willing to discover this. Be grateful to all aspects of this existence and all teachers, both the unhelpful and the very helpful. For indeed, there are loud and scary forces that exist. But they are not as debilitating as the quiet, encompassing slug of boredom and limitation sitting upon your being. So, unhook yourself. Be bigger than all of it. Say, "I am an infinite being of awesome vitality. The freeing vast winds of Oneness are with me. Grander and grander knowingness is my birthright. I hereby discard what is often perceived as unforgivable. I hereby discard that which is propelled by judgment, by the continuation of the game of shame. I discard it."

Know that you are so loved. We are with all of you as you are both delighted and troubled by this teaching. We are not here to scare you. We are here to ask you to be a part of forgiveness and love. You have come too far to reject the choice to pass the test and see yourself with loving eyes. Rhammah notices the layers of weight in the collective and does a dance. We massage the room's energy, massaging the minds and taking the attention on a mind trip while we hold all that you are in the light of love. Infinite love is all there is. And it is never separate from you. All ideas that imply otherwise need to be dismissed. Congratulations on finding this wisdom. Rhammah is impressed by all of you and bids thee adieu.

PART TWO

DIVINITY

THE LOTTERY

For You, to pick up a body in this incarnation
is indeed like winning the lottery

For You, to find this universe, this planet
is indeed like winning the lottery

For You, to shoot a blow dart thru a small ring and you win
is indeed like winning the lottery

For You, to not waste your life on unconscious behavior
is indeed like winning the lottery

For You, to own your gift to the universe
is indeed like winning the lottery

For You are on a great quest to know your own divinity
To play your part in this grand Game of Life

Discourse 1: Manifesting the Divine in Human Form

Even Rhammah has no complete way to explain how the essence of infinity and infinite love was able to collapse and individuate into a human body. We can say this. In contemplation, Oneness densifies its energy from the infinite field of love to become creation. From that point Allness moves forward, evolving and knowing itself as divinity, knowing its source and its greater nature while being in form. For that to occur, there must first be a separation, a belief in a Divine, in a Heaven which puts things into a future. That truth is allowed to be, a great creation on the crest of Allness. And it moves in an evolutionary capacity with the ability on this planet to become Human.

So, for you to pick up a body is like winning an amazing lottery. The odds for you to find this planet, for you to even find this Universe in the many universes of infinity is astounding. How one soul finds a body and a playground is no small feat. Imagine that a sea of tribal people could fit shoulder to shoulder on this continent. They would each have a very magnificent blow dart shooting to be the one to fit their dart into a ring in the distance. (*Rhammah takes a ring off the Host's finger and holds it up to demonstrate the example.*) At the count of three all these people shoot their blow guns, and the individual who scores wins a body and a journey on this planet. Considering those odds, why would you squander your lives and waste them on unconsciousness behaviors? Yet, you are free to explore this density and even to be lost in it if you choose. For in the belly of creation there are folds of darkness which are also of divinity.

However, to know the great truths and be here is a powerful quest. In such a quest you have to move out of your inclination to be lost in self-obsessions and move into knowing your own divinity. But, there is a dilemma in your experience that does not allow you to see the full connection between the infinite and the finite. You understand this quest in the person who appears spiritual. But you wonder how it works in an ignorant schlep, a slug on a couch or a sore on the spine of society. You wonder how that is a gift to the All. We say, if that is your job do it, but turn up the gusto. For one needs to own their gift to the Universe. Perhaps there are those who need to surrender their attachments and judgments. That surrendering can be their enlightenment. If so, the schlep or slug is gifting that other with the need to turn inward. Some beings volunteer to play out the role of being impossible on the behalf of another. And they are programmed by the Universe to do just that. They have signed up, perhaps won the lottery to play that part in this game.

We want you to know that you are all loved, infinitely so. Every schlep your eyes have ever seen, every slug on the couch, every miserly creature is loved. That is the way of Divinity. Of course it loves the saintly and the good. But that lovingness exquisitely, joyously also loves the angriest tyrant, the most wretched soul, every destructor, every nagger and bragger. That Infinite Divine only knows how to love. What rolls through and flows through your body, that essence is what divinity is. It is love and that is what you are. Is comprehending that a problem or a challenge for you? Love can take many forms. It often manifests as the relentlessness to stay on course, especially for the good of family, friends and society. Doing right, staying on task to assist coming generations, that is a natural embodiment of divine love. It is not a problem or challenge to be that. Indeed, it is not, not, not.

I would like to say that many more times. However, we need to get to the next point which is that you cannot not be what you are.

You cannot separate yourself from life's essence. And you are divine, inseparably so. Being that is no challenge or puzzle. It is an inevitable fact that you can relax about. Trusting is simply allowing something to be true. It's like knowing quite naturally that the sidewalk will be under your feet when you barge out your door. It is there and you know it in your belly. You are loved unconditionally. And every gesture done in that knowing defines your loving divinity. It is a great resonance, a great lift to every morsel in the environment, every splinter of wood, every molecule of glass and bit of flesh. Every morsel of an object's energy is lifted by the aliveness of what you are.

So be drunk in a childlike innocent wonder of it all. Be drunk knowing that life is at work and that its divine importance is a fact you can resonate with. Own it like you own the sidewalk under your feet when you march, like you own the seat you put this body upon. It is time for you to know, so put that before all else. Divine love is tireless. It is all powerful and you have the capacity to not doubt your power. Of course you are allowed to ignore your power if you choose. And you will still be loved. But why miss such a great opportunity? To emerge as an aspirant, you need a proclamation of undeniable, unflappable, infinitely stable facts. And even if you doubt them, you are still infinity and you will never end, not ever.

Understand that the boundaries of your body, and the boundaries between individuals and family members are all lies. Some refer to this as the illusion. And the human organism is designed perfectly to believe this falsehood. So, in order to grasp this greater identity, you must relax the offerings of the human mind. Relax and realize that when you look with divinity at what animates the body, someone like the grocer or the store clerk or the station attendant floors you with their integrity. As you see with this love, deep emotions run through the body. And, when this is not known the shadows of judgment or discontent can creep in. So say to yourself, "I am that Infinite Love. I abide in it. I call on it to be with me, to guide me, to inflate each moment with aliveness and grace. I call on this loving power and insist on its presence to shock me out of complacency, depression and apathy. These cannot exist when I know the truth that I am Eternal Love."

Now ask yourself if you could dare to stay with such a Truth even as a burglar robs you? Humans can have that opportunity. No other animal can explore the range that humans can. You can be tormented by an event in your life and allow that event to destroy your happiness. You might see a therapist for 50 years trying to re-solve issues. But you can also take shocking, challenging, traumatic events and look them square in the eye. You can look lovingly right into them and heal them. You have the range, the capacity to release, uplift and heal. And you are completely allowed the full range of experiences.

So you can choose to be a schlep, or to take on this teaching, or any choice in between. There is nothing wrong with whatever you choose. But your outcomes will be determined by your choices.

The next wave of organisms on this planet, the next evolution of humanity will be amongst those who can embrace this next step in consciousness. There will be those who say, "I am that loving divine nature that animates all life. I choose to see that nature in the burglar, in my perpetrator, in my angelic child and in the clerk at the grocery store." You are the ones contemplating this capacity and un-derstand the instructions to write your own truth. Embrace the undeni-able fact that you are limitless, loving eternity forever. Be in this grace and dismiss apathy with a passion. Dismiss being complacent. But also know that it's not wrong to refuse this teaching. This is the paradox within this play of humanity, this dance on Earth that is divine creation.

But consider your choice and consider saying, "I am that infi-nite love. I call forth this loving blessing and allow it to naturally pour forth to those I know. I am that loving power, that Divineness and I hold in love every piece of this great dream." That is the voice of the thrilled winner of the lottery ticket, of the one who really values winning a human embodiment. Keep affirming that, "I am this Divine. I cancel out the thinking that I am only this human. I relax that small sense of being and stay true with the fact that I am all of life." Be like the captain of a ship holding true, staying with his destiny through the storms, through the turbulence, through the winds. Seasoned sailors are anchored in a place that cannot be rocked, for they have seen their life flash before them so many times that all there is, is that sense of holding true. They are so stable, that solid ground does not offer more solace than the sea. When you know what you are, an easy day does not need to offer solace, for you are eternally solace.

What would it take in order to stay true to this? How would you live if it was time to stay true? Whatever that is do not forget, "I am life, I am that blessing." And it is possible to lift the whole of humanity by speaking love into every rafter of your home. You can lift humanity by holding a cup of tea and being with the Divinity that has made life possible. Or you may join a fellowship and help those in need. You can also be that blessing as you show up for work, check on your fellow or win the lottery. Any of these can be the conduit as you embrace this Truth. Divinity affirms everything for it has been embraced by your attention and your existence. As Rhammah leaves, look into what you have crystallized and create the medicine that heals despair and confusion. Cancel out whining, meanness, fear, dreariness and depression.

You are being held like an infant in the belly of the Universe. Rhammah is looking lovingly upon you, so look upon yourself with that same gentleness and acceptance. For you are Rhammah and I am you. Don't try to reason this out, embrace it! Puzzling to find the right answer is now replaced with, "I will know when I need to know." Getting answers is replaced with, "This is the way it is until it changes." For what moves is grace, and all of you are of this grace which animates the dream. It takes time to know and apply tools of knowing, so stay true with what is truly unswerving. You are allowed to take lifetimes if you need them. But this masterfulness is right here with you. You have the opportunity to simply move into it now, to be it now as its truth is given to you. Behold this dream. It is such a blessing to be with you, my brothers, my sisters, my beloved own self. You have called and I have come, gladly. Bless you.

BE IT

Pray to the one and be it

Ask the source and be it

Give it all up and be it

See it as ultimate cause and be it

Straighten out the energy and be it

Ask for the power in you and be it

Ask your highest nature to come forth and be it

Just Be It!

Discourse 2: I Give Myself to the One

Allow Rhammah to represent a visitor answering your highest questions. And do not cease to ask questions of the Ultimate Source. Rhammah represents that, and Rhammah is that and so are you. By studying this wisdom, you are in training to be a representative of the One. So, pray to the One and be it. These two concepts will confuse most spiritual aspirants, but we've decided to take that paradox on. Now, ask Source and be source. Give it all up and see it as the ultimate cause. Source is animating all and you are that source. Humbly give yourself to it as if you are willing to allow your knees to bleed. And at the same time be the absoluteness of that reality. Rhammah delivers this clean, even hand from the Absolute. I give you the truth and in doing so I straighten the energy.

The help of many masters is about you. They are the many hands of the One Source. These friends you didn't even know of are speaking to you now. They are holding you up and giving you insight. This is help from the Infinite as you are in place to aim for it and get out of your personal way. It puts you in a totally different place and yet the same exact place as always. A spiritual aspirant might ask, "How do I feel better? How do I handle the trouble that has come upon me today?" Answers are given and each answer is a half answer. It works and it doesn't because the human experience is playing one heck of a trick on you. The reason behind this conundrum is that it keeps you going. If you had all the answers, life wouldn't keep dancing. So the mind-body organism is set up to survive and thrive. Your questions and what seems important come from that set up.

Rhammah is helping you sense the stage that you are playing on and the reality behind its scenery. We help you understand a greater context. For when your answers are half answers, and then the other half of that is answered, you go to a different orbit. How do I handle my money situation or how do I handle this and that? You ask such things over and over. We say, put your qualities on the table, serve, join community, have vision, be an uplifting force and move past yourself. Each authentic answer takes you to a new and greater orbit. In a spiritual journey, you are taking your own personal reality and noticing its connection to humanity. You've moved into the orbit of humanity. There is the same crap as twenty years ago, but now it's representing humanity instead of you. You may feel ennobled, but spirituality is not a cure. It is a training to be more noble.

All of your fear, your trouble and your inner work becomes a way to be a champion of all humanity. Think of those who go through what they go through in the public eye. Athletes who have personal issues are focused upon in your media. They are taking their personal troubles and working them out on a public stage. Knowing that we are all in this together helps take the edge off. Ultimately it takes you into non-resistance, being ennobled to take on whatever is necessary. Embrace the tensions of the day and ask for the power and greater energies in you to come forth. In the beginning of this process there is the tendency to be lost, to feel confused and bumped around with big problems. By hearing about or reading about life changes, you begin to move into a greater capacity to function, a greater freedom and balance. It gets easier in time. Know that you can ask for the power in you, the Lord of Your Being to come forth.

This Lordliness is everywhere. But for Lordliness to fully animate, actualize and function through a human vehicle, that vehicle's energies and realities need to be readied and primed. Most often there needs to be some desire from your being. For the actualizing of God in form to occur, great action and authentic harmony must be cultivated. There needs to be a desire to have structure and a principled way of contemplating. For example, when relationship troubles come up, the principled commitment to love carries you through. It resists the temptation to think or say things like, "I am sick of this person. Let's give them a dig. Let's retaliate in some way." Principle keeps you from being enticed by your boredom, by your lower energies and ego attachments. Such energies do emerge for they are in the sedentary dimensions of your nature. Resist the temptation of lower energies. The principle, the vision and the structure of living in your nobility give you a safer place. They are a comfortable arena in which to stretch your use of higher energies and higher principles.

It stands to reason that a constructive vision of your personal reality and its gifts needs to be in place. Embrace your gifts enough that these traits and positions of greater harmony can be alive in you. When you give your whole self to a piece of art, or a piece of music, or an excursion in the woods you experience principle. Carry this gift of circumstance into your daily life by applying principles again and again. You often have fully developed souls who are prime vehicles for Source to utilize. So, if you desire to be a channel, join life. Use your intellect. Get both hands on creative tasks. Do not abandon your world. Rather, ask for your highest nature to come forth in your daily life. Exhibit principled integrity in even the most difficult situations. This is how you graduate, for the heavens are realized in you as they come out from you, as they are seen before you. Trust that this reality is available. Know that life's purpose can join the Oneness fully. The forces in you can handle the challenges of the modern era showing you the way.

These forces can give you clarity and power. Less attachment equals greater function and greater authenticity. In this human dance, layers and pieces of the great truth can be discovered and utilized. The dormant areas in your being are dormant because you're not ready and don't want activation. You are attached to treasured modes of being. Face the fact that humanity is full of modes of being that are treasured, that people prefer to be in. People think that if they don't have to grow and everything happens their way it's a good day. This is the mantra of humanity. You can have compassion for it because it is also in you. On some level all human traits are in you, all criminal behavior and all saintly behavior. All of the great minds and all of the wretched souls from all of history are inside of you. This is your dream and I dare you to own it.

Those who are courageous enough to face this shadow side of humanity in themselves and experience life through it ignite a fire within. It burns its way through their system and through that which is misaligned. For humanity is immersed in misalignment. You can ennoble yourself to own it and shift it. Own all appearances, those on the TV and in the person across the room. Own the human tendency to exaggerate, to embroider and embellish. Own being aggressive, intimidating, shameful and acting like a victim. They are tricks that you all have in your being. Seek development through elevated and serviceable actions, by doing heroic deeds and having noble moments of function. It doesn't have to be big, sweeping actions. Perhaps you have a moment where you did not take something so personally. Perhaps you rose above something or stayed in the zone of being principled. Look for the small opportunities what prepare you for greater actions from time to time.

At the end of the day you can unhook yourself and watch all the occurrences. This is the place that Rhammah knows so well, where all phenomena are of the One. The wretched and the saintly, the horrific and the magnificent are all seen in the distance. They are reflections on the water. At the end of the day it is time to know your eternal self which is unbounded freedom and greater function in eternity. Figuring how to hold that space and also dance in this world is the ultimate awesome responsibility of being in a human vessel. You are the dream character and also the magnificent One. It is all unfolding continually, so how does the dream character relate to it being all a dream? How do those two come together? The fact is truly they are not two things. This simple and complex paradox is easy to move beyond, so easy that it is incredibly difficult. It is closer than the nose on your face. For all that unfolds from Source, from the very first thought, it is created with the potential to discover the singularity of form and Oneness.

That potential is awakening in the human. It is emerging and there are those who would contemplate this in their life. They join and participate in such a way that they are a part of it. More and more people are allowing this to germinate in their energy and re-wire their brain, their physiology, rewire everything. Allow yourself to be prepared. But know you are participating in the very agonizing process of creating that which will fall apart. The alignment of prin-ciple sets you up for a creation that collapses. Each shift is like one draft before the next consumes it. It is one do-over and then another. The substance of your original blank slate somehow stays together enough to allow for a matrix of creations. Those are collapsing, rec-reating, then collapsing and recreating again. They are evolving into greater complexity, greater genius, greater everything. And greater means things that the current human construct can't relate to. You have no place for it. You don't know its value. There is what you think you want. But that is way off course to the Lord of Your Being and its directive. Would you dare work to stay in the alignment of your true being?

The human dance is remarkable. The infinite intelligence can take all the material that is left lying all about from a total break-down. Then it creates magnificent, beautiful newness. When you ac-cept this fact, you can laugh and allow the collapsing more easily and spontaneously. That is a normal manifest vibration, many collapses and many shifts. Those who resist it create, soar, collapse, then crash and hit the ground. It is agonizing. If your life is like that with exquisite pain from head to toe, then you have been creating with great attachment. You've been trying to hold something together that was meant to fall apart long ago. And you have layers of confusion that you need to experience like a fever. You are being shown another way, how to constantly realign to the infinite dance, to the principle of the Absolute which is even and flowing.

To allow God to show up in the front seat is generally an incremental shift. But you will find that the divine evenness maintains even if there is a roller coaster like situation. For you have within you what is unmovable and stable in your growth towards knowing. You can discover a principled quality that guides you through your relationships and your choices. And guess what, this matter you are perplexed about today won't matter in a hundred years. You won't even think of it. Your eternal self can barely even think of it now. If you are lost in troubles, that is how far away your eternal self is from you. Yet it is far away only by only a fraction, only a perception. And the concept of faraway is actually a non-truth, for your eternal self is everywhere present. Those who have affection for this fact often have been through enough and find it is time to live in total freedom.

So, what is it like to have a day where there is no activity, no excitement and yet somehow there is an ecstatic power present in your body. That power slows all of life down so that every drop of the moment seems so incredibly alive. You are drunk with noticing how exquisite everything is, every pore, every pimple, every hair, every blade of grass and all of the colors. Eternity consciousness knocks back worry consciousness. It knocks back the gripping to make one's life better, to change it, to evolve it. These get knocked back, pushed to the side and filtered through. Some people sit studying wisdom for years or lifetimes before connecting to such truth. It can vary depending on what it takes to sift through one's body of memory and one's concept of individuality and attachments. A person must go through that to find what's in harmony with and what serves their own eternity.

What in your day today will matter in a hundred years? It will be that you lived in principle and that you did at least some work to maintain evenness. You got over yourself. It won't be your accomplishments or if people noticed you. But certain events do show you eternity consciously. On the world stage there are inspiring reflections of that greater reality created. You have people sweating, acting nobly and using their gifts in alignment with their eternity. How you use your gifts is aligned with the greater arc of what you are. And you are the rarest jewel, for you know you are lifting humanity not only now, but for all time. A life lived in alignment with Eternal Source changes humanity. To sweat through your values and your treasured modes of being is why you come here time and time again. And there is a dance with what you embrace, a testing out of what is most important. It is necessary to look into your life now and ask for insight, demanding that you live intuitively. Wake up early and meditate on that. Bring your whole heart to each day and discover the genius of insight.

Such intuition is designed into creation, for the One in its infinite power gave birth to the many. The originating thought of Allness had in it a part that can see itself as the One and also mediate in a finite context. A mind-body organism can be prepared, developed, tested, and primed in such a way that grace animates it and makes way for the ultimate potential. Hear this and reflect on it. Keep this as a primary interest and live this vision authentically. Create, be engaged and insist that your activities are in alignment with your eternity. If you don't insist on it, you are not fully living. Rather you are reinforcing treasured modes of being, pockets of safety and dead ends that lead to trouble and then more trouble. Being lost in your lower nature is all right. All humans do it and can be in that cycle of repetition indefinitely. But evaluate if that is what you want.

Assessing the confusion brings the light of honestly. It is more easily done on a hilltop on a sunny day or in a circle like this with a challenge from a teacher. This is your current hilltop. Get yourself ready, then go back into the city, back into the world of activity and community living those higher qualities to the best of your ability. Amongst humans of lower nature, be honest that you are one of them. Be honest that you are also the One. When you see a hot, red-faced aggressive man who burns with pain and can't let things go, remember you are of the same nature. However, it is the lower nature, one part of two aspects. And you can be free while amongst the egos of this world.

Having a friend like Rhammah is a real trip, for it is a confirmation that you are more than the body. When the Host can leave, the Host is understood as not a body. And Rhammah is not a body except for the illusion of entering his. When you leave the body you are given choices. You are given a choice to have experiences very similar to your likes and experiences in the material world. But the sense of distance and separateness is offered, for it is often what you can handle. You leave the body and you do a small shift so it feels very similar. That is a gift from the Oneness. It is necessary. When you leave the body, there are also levels where the barriers are lessened. An experience of Oneness seems to be emerging on one level, and it is greater on the others. Here in this room you also are being offered a reality of feeling somewhat separate. And you are being offered a reality where the boundaries are gone. To one degree or another there is just the Oneness.

This experience is the holodeck of you leaving this body in this life. It's preparation and training for that time. You are contemplating the many, the One and the various dimensions of how that is put together in a matrix. There are universes, worlds set up so perfectly that infinite intelligence can play out in many aspects so the appearance of form is just so. These bodies appear in just this way, in all that they are from guts to bone to skin, to eyes, brain and muscle. And all of its ingenious ways and infinite intelligence is on the head of a pin within the infinite context. Worlds are set up in just such a way with infinity as the backdrop. Sit with that thought and you will begin to get how much of a miracle you are. The chances of you being here are a miracle and so is all that had to come into play for you to be here. If you get that, of course you would touch the hand of God with yourself as the other hand of God. You would be so present and appropriate about the body being a vehicle for the Absolute. It would be so easy to not let any treasured mode of being interrupt. And the Absolute would express itself freely. You desire that and that reality is tickling areas of your consciousness. It is destiny and you may become willing participants to some degree or another. We are all very impressed by you. Give yourselves a caring moment, the one touching the One. Be devoted. Give yourself to the One and be the One.

SOURCE

Simply begin

Find a thread… follow it back to Source

Begin with a craft, like painting, writing, or music

Let creation pour through your hand… come forth from your lips

All of life in a poetic dance

Rest inwardly… discovering all of creation is of Source

You can call it… love, or creation, or yes

Find just one thread and go home with it

So much peace... so much power... so much creativity

Discourse 3: I Rest in Beloved Source

You often compare one teaching to another. For some, this can lead to confusion. Your mind thinks, "How does this teaching compare to the other? How does a profound, nonlinear presentation relate to a teaching that is good medicine for a tough moment?" The various teachings of the many faiths and spiritual teachers are for different contexts that dance in the various presentations of you. Understand that a teaching is simply a beginning where you follow its thread to the Source. Know that your energies are painting on so many levels. To become unified in yourself, find a space where you know the most important thing is to dismiss confusion and be in stillness. To elevate you must dismiss the game of trying to figure it all out.

So, rest as what you are, as the very Source of Being. Then a natural sense of how to be and what to do will come from your pores, from your very own natural state. But your mind might say, "I am not there yet. That is not how I do things. That is not how I have done things." Although the mind may say that, here in this room it is time to know. So, rest and be still in the beloved Source. The strength and velocity of your many stories will lessen as you merge into this Source. Imagine how that looks. It is a very vital, rich dynamic knowing. Source sits on the stump right where you are, and I am asking you to relax with and be with it. It knows in ways that might not completely satisfy the human. But if the human falls for it, there is so much peace. This Source is the creative energy that one experiences through their craft, their talent or skill. You find it in those moments of joy that are felt when the wind blows through the trees. That is creation and the power of it all becomes more and more obvious. You will sense it in the simplest things. For example, the dog chasing a stick becomes creation. The child flying a kite and even the lovers quarreling become it. For one experiences the awesomeness of all things, knowing they are the presentations of the Source which you are. Your own creativity is of that Source. So pull out the paints, write a poem, do a craft project or write a letter from your heart. Whatever works, you can start there. Use this teaching to understand that creation pours through your hand. It comes forth from your lips. It is all of life in its poetic dance. Do whatever it takes to experience the magnificence of creation. Rest inwardly and discover that all of creation is of Source.

How about getting quiet enough that you hear your heart beat in your ear drum or you experience the awesome rush of blood through your body as your heart pulses. It is obeying Source in its unending power, obeying its unending brilliance and its magnificent ways. You can call it love. You can call it Yes. You can call it Source. You can call it creation unfolding and dancing. Find a way, find just one thread and go home with it. And if your own internal environment feels pinched or dense or troubled in some way, we tell you this. Asking conflicted questions about differing wisdoms is like rubbing two threads together. Just pick one or the other. In truth they are the same. So say yes to them all existing. Contradiction and differences are just part of being fully human.

Meanwhile, unfettered love is saying yes completely to how humans are, to how you are. Whatever is dense, twisted, stale, stiff, aching, or unmoving, look at it. Hold it and say yes. Rub its belly and laugh into it. For Source is everywhere presenting itself as everything. There are very tricky and confusing forces in human consciousness. There are also very magnificent and brilliant forces inviting your minds into freedom. Those forces are playing in the sciences, in books, in literature. These scriptures and visions of gods that exist around your planet and exist in human consciousness are ingenious and elaborate in many ways. There are divine beings who work in various ways so that humans can be attracted to realms beyond their usual contraction. For the natural limitation of being a human sets up a sense of being completely myopic. It is a conundrum to be human. And in many ways for many of you it is the intellect that snares you, that creates trouble.

Because this is so, we speak of geometry and dimensions as a way for you to see the parameters in your environment. You can see the angles. You can see around things. But then, when we add more dimensions to your mind, it begins to stop and you move out of the pull of being only human. You have the capacity to expand towards the creative Source. Often the human craves another exciting piece of intellectual poetry to entice this vulnerability, to lure its genius. And many of the helper beings enjoy artists and writers for they have more sensitive, refined feelers hanging out in their consciousness. When the divine ones approach them, they are willing to ruminate. They are more likely to sense that there are realities beyond what can easily be expressed, or easily imagined.

Are we often speaking about things that you are not supposed to understand? Yes, we are. Are we throwing things at you so your minds hang out in openness? Yes, indeed. You have the notion of what is phenomenal in your world. You can look upon any aspect of natural beauty and find the phenomenal. It is a phenomenon when the winds of the Divine blow through your field and the sails are full of those winds. Feeling open and powerful and with the higher forces, with the divine ones is so phenomenal. The potential of all phenomena allows for the whole of all experiences. And there are multiple dimensions that can be experienced in your mystical practices. Some of you can be quiet and go on journeys. You can expand and sense other dimensions. Those dimensions which you come in touch with, the ones you converse with and have insights with, they are phenomenal.

The capacity to see visions and to experience acute visual phenomena is of vital importance in so many ways because it is like medicine. You have a cough so you take cough medicine. You are struggling with your career and you need insight. You have a migraine and you need the discovery of healing power, or perhaps an aspirin. Whatever it is, there are ways of dancing in phenomena that are naturally preferable. But while you work and play in the realm of phenomena, know that somewhere in you nothing is as important as you think it is. And when one is ready to go for the highest, one dismisses all the phenomena. You say, "Thank you for hell, I dismiss it. Thank you for heaven, I dismiss it. I am going directly to Source." You might say, "I've had a rolodex of spiritual insights flutter through this brain that must be enlightened, and none of them are the answer."

When you have discovered what you are, it is helpful to note that there is a "YES" that does not go away. At first a deep contraction happens in yes, but it only plays out for so long. Then, in quantum fashion, a bliss state appears. And there is no preferred experience in the "YES" of this bliss state. That is freedom, having no preferred experience. From the perspective of "No Preferred Experience," if I know I'm destined to go to Mexico, I will start on a track towards Iowa. Right? (*There is group laughter.*) Or you may go up across the other direction of the planet, taking the long trip. If you are oriented to go for it at some point, this is a good teaching for you. It will guide the preliminary stages of your development. On your way to disappearing into non-phenomena, you must know about the realms of phenomena. Realizing this, you handle each day in such a way that you relax about the various phenomena that appear. There is no longer the micro-managing, and a naturalness settles in.

The Source of all that appears has to be before and below the phenomena that are its presentations. This teaching is a rudder that gives you more power than you initially might think. For wellness is way more a possibility. Coming out of a bad mental state is way more of a possibility. You do not take things so seriously and neither do you take relief so seriously. For relief is just a natural event in phenomena. When the universe's intelligence is allowed to cohabitate in your energy fields, in your minds and your consciousness, you become vulnerable to a reality that is beyond reality. When you are able to trust what you cannot touch, see, taste, smell or fathom with intuitive perception, you are very vulnerable. And in that state, you are opening yourself to be taken care of by the highest, grandest and most monumental of forces.

When this happens it becomes more and more fun to be a dream character and to have victories. It is natural to have a victory. And when it is all understood as just a play, the presentation of courage alongside fear is seen in the right light. They create each other and in the full play of events, of course the hero wins. This is how all phenomena work. One hero sits next to an aspiring hero. She has a story. She has a struggle. We can all relate and we want to see the happy ending. In limitation this gets dicey. But in the greater knowing of what we are, victory absolutely can exist. You will say, "I have an unconditional respect for this moment and my role in it and my capacity to bring greater and greater love to what presents itself." What a grand story it is to ask oneself, "What happens when I take on the tasks I am given this day with a bigger heart? What can happen if I bring more of what I am to this day?" So, look into the matters of the day head on. Get under them. Bring infinite love forth.

Doing this is easy for Rhammah. Rhammah knows itself like water that falls down the mountain and finds itself rushing in a river. That water falls into the various places offered by the mountainside, the valley and eventually moving on to the sea. I am like that water.

And like that water, my knowing pours into all of your worlds excellently.

Whatever you are doing is so equally interesting to Rhammah, and the waters that run forth are offered equally. All of your adventures are so interesting and so worthy that in my world there is no concept of more or less, better or worse. Could you own that? Would you dare own that as a practice? Live in the integrity of that truth and bring more of yourself to any and every moment that presents itself. That is awakening.

So, as you discover creation through your vessel, you will begin to discover all of creation and everything becomes poetry. All of it, the breath moving, the sounds from your neighbor and the hum of a machine in the next room are its components. Screaming children become like a song. The lawnmower outside your meditation room, your mother and your father are all seen as texture in creation. Enjoy them as you are discovering this awakened life. Discover a real spirituality, a real one. Isn't that what you want, a real spirituality and not something phony? Watch how the doors open. When you are living in your own hell, it is a phenomenon, is it not? And of course it is time to experience the other side of that in manifest form. But it does help to have the compass set for the greater awakening. When you take care of this truth and cultivate it in yourself, it is a benefit to your family, your friends and all whom you connect with.

In a harmonious field, the higher realms play through that being. When a word is spoken, those sounds becomes vehicles for the gods. They can get in the ear and vibrate through a being transforming it. If you desire to be a seed planter, you must study your energy and how you take care of yourself. Consider carefully how you stage what you say, and how you stage how you are. We are delighted to share this understanding with you. The healing gifts of this evening are also benefitting the Host. That he has given this time to you by allowing me to come through, he is benefitting also. As you all heal he is healing with you. Bless you. Rhammah bids thee adieu.

NOTICE

Notice how the universe conspires to help you

Notice the genius of spirit

Notice how the universe conspires to work things out

Notice the insights you gain

Appreciate your breakthroughs

Love yourself into this new adventure

Live in humility, remaining approachable and available

Notice and be balanced with buoyancy, resilience and alignment

Simply Notice

Discourse 4: Loving the Vessel and Insisting on Truth

Why not appreciate your vessel in the same way I do the Host's vessel? Why not see your vessel in the light of magnificence? Do this like one who is quivering in young love or passionate for an ambition. There are those who are touched by the sound of a violin, touched by great artists or those inspired by angelic forces in your world. Humans are moved by such expressions. We are asking you to see the magnificent vehicle which you reside in as you would a sacred song. It is a gift to you, a magnificent opportunity. Being able to form and capture thoughts gives it the ability to do what it does. And in that ability, great issues arrive because of the biological imperative to survive and thrive. Most often this biological imperative has a competitive nature. It has competitive energy in it. And because of that, you will not be able to spiritually evolve without cultivating love for yourself and others.

It is good to wake up and deliberately bring love to your human vessel, turning on all its capacities. Can you imagine a master walking through a wall? Their physical body would transform into brilliant light so high in frequency that it matched the electron patterns of the wall and passed through them. Similarly, imagine a master knowing they are infinite love and being in that high frequency. They could do what is even more important than passing through a wall. Such a master would be able to move through all of this world's weight, limitation and turmoil. The bulk of the negative would roll off them. If one has that alignment, they are alive with the blessings of the Infinite. Ignite your form consciously with such love and with the goal of it becoming automatic. You will see glimpses of this as you practice. It doesn't mean you become impervious to the issues of others. More importantly, your gentleness does not go away. It is just that you are no longer affected by the weight of the world's stuck energy.

Being in such a blessed space is a thrill of sorts. You may watch the minds of others flicker in their own shadow until they cannot use the heaviness and it falls apart. This is an evolution and observing it becomes a thrill, for you know they are waking up. Those affected by being in your divine space may be afraid of their own light. But you see deliverance, for they are being tested by the light of divinity. There is nothing more brilliant and wonderful than to partake and to be a part of this power. This alive, knowing force is completely available. Its substance animates the whole dream and your very own being. You can own it as your own self. Do this through dismissing limitations and by affirming the lordliness that is everywhere. Affirm it as self and that, yes you are indeed infinite love.

Your human vessel is designed perfectly to be run by that love and to be inhabited by it in a very natural way. The more natural and less postured you are, the more power there will be. At the heart of your being, an atomic, brilliant awareness is ready to blast off. It can blast you into vast, awesome freedom. So, insist on discovering and actualizing that capacity. It is your birthright as a divine being who inhabits a divine vessel. For the vessel is completely divine, and it is your job to make sure it is seen that way. Be with every part of your body from head to toe, every hair and pore and wrinkle.

Own it as magnificent divine love, holding your being in the light of your own Lordliness. Be with your body like a young lover yearns to be with her partner, like a mother yearns to be next to her babe.

Do not let up on the potential of vitality, the potential for health and for transformative breakthroughs. Reach for this and do not be a sissy about it. We mean it! Your brain can be rewired and your body can be alive and active. You can dismiss depression and apathy by affirming the Lord of Your Being. Say to yourself, "I insist on this alive presence and this infinite intelligence and this divine love to be completely present. I insist that it inhabits this vessel and its reality appears in everything I look at. All that I look upon seems like gold. All that I hear seems like gold, for it is divinity." Essentially this is so while your life plays out as a very elaborate game of smoke and mirrors. The simplicity of aligning to the reality you are and insisting on it to be present is the stuff of awakening. So, why not affirm divinity and dismiss limitation? Dismiss the flickering, illusionary, shimmering, complex trickiness that is human conditioning.

As you affirm the boundless reality, relax into the great soup of love that goes on forever. Each human vessel is the head of a pin that all of the Infinite is dancing upon. It dances even as you participate in a finite game. So, live your life as if it is a masterpiece. Be willing to tell your story to others and allow them to join in on your play. You are the hero in your own challenge, alive to watch patterns and discover the limits in your story. It's okay to admit that you have been a piece of work. There is so much courage in that. It is so well appreciated and inspiring. The game of I can do this and I can do that can be hard to slow down. But life finds its way to help you see. After all, here you are in this circle striving to see your current circumstance in a greater light. And some of you deliberately engage with viewing things in a new way, a preferred orientation.

As you align with this practice, notice how the universe conspires to help you work things out. You can magnify how that works and strengthen the genius of the universe as you notice its spirit. It is alright to be honest about a deep, deep pattern that will not budge. Be honest with your fellows and speak of it. Better yet, be in a place where you are willing to gain insight on how to be with your pattern and how to work with it. You are being asked to take what you have worked on, express it and be with it as infinite love while you appreciate your breakthroughs. You must respect that there are so many who would not choose to see situations the way you do or address them in the same way. Appreciate your own viewpoints and simultaneously know they are small cracks, little chips into your infinity. Love yourself into this new adventure that you are creating. Simultaneously, live in the humility that makes you approachable, raw, crackling with growth and available. Your energy will have a luster and the motions which play through your body are allowed completely without being lost in themselves.

As masters you can be responsive and energetically supple with your environment. At the same time, you can have the high sensory capacity to be balanced with joyous buoyancy, resilience, and deliberate insistence on alignment for yourself and for life. There are some of you who have to function in a flatland environment. To speak out of the box would have deeper ramifications for you than it might have for others. Our words of wisdom can bring value to those who are a right fit. They have benefits you are both aware of or not aware of. Rhammah's wisdom might seem simple at times, however its meaning is far greater than I can give you. Few in your flatland environment may be open to this expansion of understanding. That is alright. But, consider a small act of kindness in a day spent within a flatland crew of associates. They are locked in their intellectual boxes. An act of kindness which is delivered without a point of view can be your way to deliver infinite love.

The "real self" can inwardly say, "This is a small matter. I will not let it get to me. I am profoundly brilliant. I abide in my expanded self naturally and effortlessly. What matters most to me is seeing this lifetime as a wonderful, temporary dream. I wish to discover the aliveness that permeates through the whole dream. I wish to discover that aliveness as my very own self. So even to you, my tormentor, I will be gentle and kind." You say all of that in yourself by simply being helpful in a very quiet way, often without flapping your jaw at all. These words are a scaffolding through which we intend to help you know what you are. Many words can be said, and their reality has a stunning simplicity. Truth is affirmed through being with others in a quiet, prayerful way, and being honest enough to represent your totality even in a small gesture.

You may say, "I see your struggle. I'm concerned about your heavy thinking process because I like you." Then leave it there. You may have been going to therapy groups for years. You may be committed to identifying heavy thinking and moving it out. Or it may be a lifestyle you enjoy, investing time and energy on it. That's may be what you are thinking inside of you, but you will not talk about it to this person. You may have a universe of knowing vibrating through you. Cultivate it by being real with what you are discovering and how you are living in an appropriate way. Some playwrights can put a whole world of understanding in the exchange of a few lines. Worlds of meaning are often conveyed by a short story. You can join in life in that way, representing but not outshining, not showboating or grandstanding, not trying to change people and make them better. It is enough to appreciate them in infinite love.

Light up inside by being real with your truth in a very small way. Your action may seem so small, but realize that small acts are alive with the energy of an awakened being. Transmission of that energy begins with waking up and insisting on loving your vessel like a mother loves her child. Say yes to your vessel like it is the edge of a knife that can cut through the crap of humanity, cut through the stuff of your day. Do whatever it takes. If it takes a lot of wisdom from books and writings, do it while insisting on more truth and turning up the gusto. When you realize your mind is taking you off track, be gentle in a very deliberate and emphatic way. Perhaps you can say, "Hello mind, I see you are here. Yes, you've got my attention. In fact you seem to have it all the time. While you are an awesome force, my dear mind, I must be with you in an even more loving way than I have been before. I understand you are trying to take care of me. But let's face the fact that doesn't work very well, for most of what you think is not real."

This is true because much of what you think has been affected by human conditioning. Yet, the events of daily life are of the universe, a universe that is a complete miracle. Be shocked by the fact that you can even hear. Be shocked that you can feel pain. Be completely astounded that even the most malicious, horrific dramas can appear. Be aware that in the most awe inspired way this manifest mystery inhabits your consciousness. Having an appreciation for the mystery of existence takes you to a more balanced space. When it is unnecessary or unhelpful to act, you will be more inclined to back away. You will not need the rhetoric in your head to know when to rest and when to act. For the knowing of when to act comes from a space where the energy does what it does because it feels right.

There are other types of wisdom and groups that are essentially after what you are after. It is a growing phenomenon. Sometimes it's messy when people are practicing things that are off the mark. Very often, their intentions matter more than what they are practicing. Their intention to grow into truth is there and that part is good. Then think for a moment about beings who have somehow earned the right to sit on a hilltop. They sit on a rock and do nothing and know nothing needs to be done. There are beings so evolved that their circumstances have deemed that possible. And by virtue of it being possible, it is necessary. For it is designed into the universe, and into their being and makeup, to manifest as that expression.

But then there are those who are like yourselves. Most of you here attempt to inhabit the truth that nothing needs to be done. Yet you are living lives and doing many things. You are questing inside of the energies that are alive and able to be played out, to be danced through. The desire for community, for psychological wellbeing, for greater function and happiness is just as noble as waking up completely. They are as worthy as the master on the hilltop who knows everything as just a dream. And indeed that energy, the energy of that being is holding up the whole world. So, measure yourself up against that, living life in such a way that you are not trying to fix or help from a human space. Be kind to yourself for the whole dream is yourself. Be honest and honor the energies you are given.

Perhaps you have a set of gifts that needs to manifest, like being a great organizer for example. What would humanity do without great organizers? Look at your way of working today and turn up the energy. And if you are not trying to save the world through actions, that's okay. But be kind to it and you will know that everything is different. The transformative power that you are is thrilling for you and for those around you who are ready. So, yes it can be fun to wake up. In the early days yes, it is often fun. But when the honeymoon wears off, then you find out it is not for sissies. As Rhammah, I am representing infinite love and being real about it. In the context of this dialogue you cannot know what I am completely. But you may enjoy trying to know some of what this is all about. You may wonder what kind of theater performance is playing through this Host. Let that be okay.

You can envision your existence like a forest that you get caught up in and yearn to find answers within. Then realize that there are all kinds of intelligent forces and beings at work that have been around your planet and involved with humanity for many thousands of years. They play a perfectly magnificent tricky game. They dance through the trees using the truth deceptively, tricking you into distractions of one type or another. So, deliberately call the brilliant truth in through the trees. Be clear that you want the absolute truth, not the colorized truth or the tainted truth or the slightly shifted truth. Draw the light through the trees. Do this clearly and the complexity that is the roof of the forest has to allow for this intention. Walk in truth through the forest of humanity, through its wildernesses. And know you are not alone.

What a service it would be to have more beings calling in the light, knowing absolute truth and being highly functional. Know and work with the loftiest of truths. Repeat phrases like, "I am an alive, present, aware life force. I am Godly, divine infinite love. This matter that appears on the forest floor is a very finite matter. I would be with it in a kind, appropriate gentle way as a representative, as an ambassador for the Ultimate. I am being appropriate, being real, but not too much." What you are really after is being real with all that you are and letting its effects just happen. Strengthen this ability.

You may think of your disturbing, creepy uncle like you might think of the slimy frog on the forest floor. Hold that frog in your mind and ruminate on its environment. Bring love to what you hold in mind. As you affirm your eternity, allow that frog to be what it is. In this mental exercise we do not ask you to be less than real about where that frog needs to live. The frog needs to live in dark places for it to be what it is. But you can embody what you are in such a way that you bookend the process, making sure you are staying aligned. I would ask you to represent truth, knowing that others will not get the whole truth that you know inside. So manage that well. Get good at it, for there will be more and more to do as you go along. The art of living in this truth has rich rewards. We are with you and in all respects please do insist on being with the untainted truth. Dismiss the ghosts in your trees. Rhammah bids thee adieu.

LORD OF YOUR BEING

Where might you witness the lord of your being?

Watching a sunset over the water

Writing a poem that moves your soul

Creating a painting that pleases you

Complete knowing……. affirm it……. affirm it often

Give yourself, the lord of your being, kindness and warmth

Give it to yourself and you will not need it from others

Trust the lord of your being

Discourse 5: Preparation for Big Wisdom

The Host agreed to utilize his own body organism as a vessel for Rhammah. Rhammah is a presence of love that is infinite. While that is so, Rhammah is also many masters. I am also you in the sense that we are family members of the One Source. We come here to discuss and deliver how reality exists on many levels at once. You ask questions from your human perspective and we supply answers from our infinite perspective to the degree possible. Understand that your ability to conceive of things is limited by your third dimensional experience and other human limits. Because of these limitations, some of our answers will seem like a paradox to you. For example, while there are levels, there's also no levels because Oneness in its magnificent atomic indivisibility is beyond levels. It's beyond divisions or numeric representations.

You can use contemplation to break down the mental illusion of separate identity so that you might abide in the One. You are a full embodiment of the One, as are all things. It is rare for a level of exchange, like the one Rhammah brings, to fully manifest on your planet, but this situation is gifted to you. Rhammah comes as a teacher to impart presence so that the teaching can come forth like waves of energy. Every morsel of your being, every hair on your head we prize like a father or mother would prize a child. We respect you like we would respect our very own brothers and sisters from our realm. Your autonomy, your freedom to choose messages both unwise and wise is equal in the sense that we will not love you less for your choices. You do not need to fear anything with us.

The truths we give are contemplations for this period of your time. As you are eternal beings, "this period" may mean for a series of 100 lifetimes. And we do speak to you knowing that you are in a series of lifetimes. At other times what we say may be about the next fifteen minutes or weeks of your time. The place we reference and invite you into puts no value on fifteen minutes or 100 lifetimes. Our size has nothing to do with time. We are beyond a blink of an eye and a second in eternity. The moments that we are in fellowship with you is what truly matters. They also do not matter a bit, for there is eternity. So, how does the human mind reconcile a teaching like this? We are here to help you get used to the fact that your mind will not get used to such a teaching. It is Big Wisdom and the human will not ever be completely used to Big Wisdom.

Be assured that we are here to answer your questions from a truly loving place and not to give you a rough rub or a bum steer. You are not ever judged or condemned by Source Divine. But we can see what's called for as guidance. And more often than you might think, when one is escorted into bigger wisdom the human identity is kicking and screaming. The attached ego fights its deliverance to wisdom. That is remedied somewhat in a fellowship where the energy of truth is freedom. For when one is ready, wisdom is exhilarating. It is weight off the shoulders, a chest full of fresh air, a belly full of laughter and a sense of empowerment. But know, to be prepared for the next leap in understanding there are different phases of development that are called for. It helps to be on a transition towards nobility.

The nobility of your thoughts and actions and a leaning towards a compassionate, unified vision aids your preparation. Understand that there is wisdom and then there is wisdom. In your culture there are various stages of wisdom. Not all of your established wisdoms allow for a state of no fear and total freedom. We come to examine the subtle levels, delivering that to the light. Delivering your many games and strategies to the light involves understanding full well that most games are tied up with fear and ego. Your many cultural strategies are the best that human conditioning has come up with. But you are now, at last, in direct fellowship with divine energy. We are ennobling you with the capacity to receive wisdom that is up-front, stalwart, real, upright and forthright. We are preparing you to be a decent human being, which is fine and perfect and all too often forgotten about.

To absorb and engage this wisdom totally, it is necessary to know one's own divinity fully. There are many phases in a human lifetime which prepare one for this. And there is no purpose bigger than to gain these understandings. Some are struck by seeking it earlier than others. They are called to be in a mindset where they know what is divine in them, which is also God. This is often the result of many lifetimes of preparation. When a person is ready, they know that their great purpose is to discover what they are. And there is nothing wrong with the various ways this is accomplished or worked with. Often, the instinct towards one's divinity manifests as service. One may feel called to be a school teacher, a spiritual teacher or a healer. These are great possibilities that set the stage for discovering what you really are. It actually exists within the heart of these roles. But others move into a different place with the wisdom, seeing all as service to mankind. In the most realized the greatest humility is possible. They ennoble their daily tasks. Whether that be grocery bagger, dishwasher, maid or taxi driver, the one who knows the truth does not see himself or herself as less. They do their work out of service, creating a groove for others to smile through.

You can ennoble any daily tasks with purpose, presence, kindness and knowing. You realize your divinity, knowing you are not less. Such a practice is the least valued and perhaps the most important. For does not a true leader feel a kinship with all. Those who are struggling and scraping, you feel an affinity with that because you know you are part of that. That individual is you, made of the same One Source. There should be a crisis of spirituality if a person has even a subtle narcissistic impulse towards thinking they have a more special purpose. To see yourself above anyone else, that concept is so captivating and so deceptive. It's so tempting to have grandiosity. And there are souls here who have had plenty of grandiosity for plenty of lives. And what did those soul journeys get them set up to be? They will reincarnate to be exquisitely, magnificently ordinary, completely and wonderfully unknown.

The wisdom we bring is an immense wisdom. If you knew how Rhammah sees it, you would fall into tears. You would know the humility of truth and the exquisiteness of Divinity. You would know its gentleness, its lightness, its concreteness and its strength. Are you here to desire that? You do not have to be. You can come here for any reason you desire. You might not get a lot of validation for other things. But you are loved regardless. And why not come for a good cookie and a nice blessing to set you up for a good week. There is nothing wrong with your individual identity and personality. But when the light is shining down from the highest truth, everything looks different. It may outwardly remain the same, but inwardly something is going on.

I'll have you know it is always rough to be a human. If you are given great wealth, certain things in the ego are hard to get out of. Traps that one cannot even see are given by affluent parents. But even those ones, as all are not less loved. For there are different ways that wisdom must play out in each human. Each journey needs to be embraced and exquisitely right as just so perfect. And the various circumstances give opportunities that challenge others. For example, can you have compassion for the snotty brat who goes to college, does not pay his rent and barely shows up to class? Can you love the snootiness because that human is doing the very best he or she can? In that lifetime, that one is learning affluence. In other lifetimes they were slaves. There are some lifetimes intended to give you a break. Each situation might be different. Have your imagination go off with this and stretch into the possibilities for every life lesson.

It is fun to play with this concept. Lifetime after different lifetime, exploring all the different worlds people have been in. What kind of journey are they in now? Why does that soul need this physical challenge or this illness of the body? You see it knocking them on their ass and wonder why Jesus or God doesn't give them the cure. Understand that the backgrounds of each journey may be useful in healing issues or giving that person context. Of course there can be easier ways. There are different atmospheres where renewal can happen more rapidly, for the light of your being is prior to all circumstances. A spiritual path might be imagined as an antidote to everything. You think if God is loving you, nothing bad should ever happen. Or if you are spiritual enough all will be right. However, an immobilization of one's being, be it from physical sickness or psychological trauma, can be occurring on various levels. Souls can choose hard conditions in order to learn lessons or align and balance prior actions. There are always reasons why various occurrences are happening to various souls in a given human lifetime. Why would God interfere with that?

When we come from higher levels to instruct, we try not to get tangled up with the finite dealings of human lives which might keep us from getting to the point of your divinity. The capacity to be with all that appears can be immobilizing. Everyone here knows how that happens. All of you feel stuck at times. Some of you have felt very stuck for a long time. You may be stuck energetically, psychologically or attitudinally which all evolve ultimately to spiritually. And when it is addressed as a spiritual thing, results happen in their own time. That is the alignment when you are here. Results happen on their own timeline. That is the way spiritual knowing works. Often it is played out as very practical, but often it isn't.

Where Rhammah comes from, when we speak of truth it is different than speaking of time. The reference of eternity is different than time. From the human perspective, eternity is seen as a time line reference from before forever forward into a future forever. But in spiritual sight, forever means that in each point and in between each point, the present is always infinite in its boundlessness. It is present in a way that dances in eternity. You have the sense of being locked up in the body. That is a joke being played upon you, for the truth is you are in many worlds at once. And those worlds can get discovered when you are knocked on your ass. To be taught about that can be rough, but what is in you makes it so grand. Are you in charge or is divinity within you in charge? Here we say you are that divinity that is in you. Knowing that makes it easier to adjust to whatever healing is upon you.

When we say that healing is upon you, we mean that you are being taken to your divinity. It's a breakdown of what you think should be. It's also a discovery of the vastness of freedom. If you knew yourself to be that freedom, then this paralyzing fear could be allowed and loved. It would not need to go away, for the spiritual self says, "It will move on when it moves on." Ten minutes of fear shows you eternity when it paralyzes you, when it arrests your imagination of possibilities. It takes away your whole life, that moment. But noticing the eternal dimension of that fear is noticing how Source works. Eternity has many ways it plays itself out. It can play any game. It is evident as all that is before you. Eternity and life produce a planet, vegetation, water, life, creatures in the sea, evolution and variety. Often fear is instinctual, but it can be manmade. A rabbit running from a fox is the right kind of fear. However, humans can create very troubling psychological situations as part of the dance. The capacity to notice this shows you a way to turn things around.

When the human consciously looks into life there is a reaction. This is how paradox is set up in the world of form. When the human in its plight, inside its mind worships itself, then its willfulness gets tangled up. Humans can get very tangled, experience suffering and have few breakthroughs of understanding. Spiritual truth is the only lasting remedy to such human suffering. Beings who show up to study wisdom like this get released for periods of time. That is like a pot of gold. It is a great richness to know even a little of what Rhammah speaks about. So, how does one get ready for Big Wisdom? It does help to be treated with kindness. And if that is not occurring, one must treat themselves with kindness, with compassion and cultivate love of self. All should do this.

Of course there are environments that are very difficult. Some make their way through and some don't. There are those with great strength who have made it through the worst scenarios and discovered the light within. They abide in that and it smiles out of them in spite of all. In such challenges the evolving beings might say, "Dear Lord of My Being, the willfulness of my conscious self is rubbish. I call on the Lord of My Being, that which is the light. I ask it to come forth and be with me in this situation. Dear Lord of My Being, I ask you to come forth and show me how to be with this, how to see it." This core, this spark is what is prayed for and asked for. It is lovely to envision going to a heaven after a lifetime lived well in charity. It is so lovely and delicious. You are here to be ennobled and discover that.

Such rewards can appear when you put aside the needy games, the aggressive games, the show-off posture and the attention getting. Put those all aside and in that knowing discover that what comes forth is noble. Set that action forth in the world with energy. It shakes the Earth and moves the human heart. It moves others into wanting to know. That ennobled action is alive with the knowing of the Lord of One's Being. You might witness the Lord of Your Being on the water when you are watching the sun set in the distance. The Lord of Your Being is in a poem that moves your soul. Or perhaps when painting a rabbit hopping in your back yard, there it is again. The Lord of Your Being is a palpable knowing touching you. Affirm it, affirm it often. Do what it takes for its presence to increase.

You can practice increasing this presence in various ways. For example, imagine being shouted at by the biggest, hairiest aggressive sucker in the world. You could say, "Ah, it is the Lord of My Being." There is so much love in that, although there is nothing wrong with not being at that level of truth. There's nothing wrong with having human conditioning, or being susceptible to fear. We are just suggesting the potential. How much of this are you willing to consider? Can you sense that the Lord of Your Being is present even when a friend says a silly, hurtful thing? Begin with small situations that are easier for you to master. They can be imagined or real. Then work up to bigger things. The imagined situations are okay, but eventually apply this to the real.

What time are we in, this era when catastrophe abounds? You are in the era where if you are not choosing to be with this quality of wisdom, it could be so difficult. It has been that time for quite a while. Partly being played out on the planet is how the egos have manifested themselves within countries, and from country to country. The people struggle, fight and much is destroyed. They fight to prevent a breakdown of what they believe and have known as their way. That loss can be even more frightening than the loss of communities in great catastrophes. The loss of how I think everything is, how I think I am and what I think is real is closer to home than the literal devastation of your planet. But this false identity devastation is myopic and delusional in you.

If you desire to be with your real divine nature, the chances that you will feel devastated on one level are not as great. You will have a better capacity to move on. My house is burned down, but now I can see new possibilities. That is how spirit sees it. And you can assist and mediate with the human persona like you would with a child who needs to be helped along. When your fever of fear gives you a break, can you talk to yourself lovingly like you would your child? The Lord of Your Being can touch the human self, giving it kindness and warmth. Give it to yourself and you will not need it from others. You may receive it, but not need it. Make yourself play at trusting life.

There is so much in humanity that you cling to. Much of what we are speaking about can seem like a distant song. You are entertained, it is lovely, but as you move out the door it is sort of forgotten. There is nothing wrong with that. The truth will still call you. How it is delivered to you is still there moving very slowly. It is still a delight for Rhammah that you would be so interested, so desiring of truth like a bug on a light for at least a moment. That is so right. We are also here for those who will honestly attempt to realign and be that Lordly self. It is an abstract teaching, and it needs to stay there. This is how Big Wisdom is. It does not fit between the ears. It does not fit within the confines of human conception.

You are learning a new form of personal culture, giving this mind-body organism to the energies and using its intelligence and creativity. Let it use all of that in humility, in gentleness and unstoppable clarity. Rhammah comes to encourage you, which helps entrain your self-encouragement. Encourage each other, encourage friends and family. You do not need to tell them, "I know of this man who does strange things on Saturday night. These very strange, esoteric, wild poetic things come out of his mouth. I do not recognize him when he goes into altered states. I've not got it figured out." You do not have to talk about this. It is probably preferable if you don't. You can simply sit and be with Lordly Source itself. Ask it to come forth in your life and be with your friends and your family. Ask it to guide you, being humble about the necessity of doing that continuously. Be humble with the amount of human conditioning that is working to trick you into limitation, hopelessness, despair and anxiety. Be humble that you might cut that all out at the gate.

The presence that is in all things, in your bodies, in the trees, in all of life is dancing in magnificent ways. It is supreme intelligence. It is dancing here exquisitely as all of life. Everything points the impassioned spirit towards that truth, every event. But you will discover how quickly conditioning chomps at this awareness, how it wants to get in the way of its magnificent wonder. When you see how that works, at the break of morning you can ask the Lord to be present, before the mind creates its mess upon you. You will ask it to be like the rising sun, to come forth, shine out your eyes and burst through the actions of the day. Ask it to be present in such a way that the mind cannot meddle. And do it again later, and do it again. If this is discovered for even two minutes a day, you are a very rare human. Give yourself credit, as that is so right.

A lifetime can be so difficult without this alignment. Even with it, life can still be difficult. But if the play of difficulty is seen in the light of its divine nature, it can be seen as a new way that things are right. It can become what is right with the world. For the greatest works of art that move the soul often come from your challenges. They can come from wretched acts where there are forces at play that call forth a truth. Life is an experience. It is like Shakespeare and you are in that exquisite storyline. It is a romance of the self to find yourself. Why would you want it any different? The Lord of Self says, "Ah, this is all so delicious." Infinite love is all that we see when we come. We see the different ways infinite love plays out, even in difficulties and often beneath all that is appearing. There is this capacity to abide with that. And, know you the classic way of abiding? The truth is stillness. Silence is its highest expression. Bless you, Rhammah bids thee adieu.

PART THREE

HUMAN GROWTH

VIBRATING WITH LIFE

Take a difficulty and use it, be ennobled through it

Lean into the unknown

Find a way inside yourself to say yes

Change your life from the inside out

Point yourself toward eternity

Embrace the life you choose

The great sea of energy is in every drop of your being

Vibrate with it

Discourse 1: Balancing the Dimensions of Density

(This discourse addressed questions about natural preservation, politics and the nature of evil.)

You all have a passion for thinking and everyone here yearns to know. You are also willing to rethink significant issues. There are various ways of knowing and various dimensions to knowing. Can you work with yourselves so that you become knowing itself, the knowing quality that is of life? You now have ways to measure how much the body weighs and what the blood pressure and quality of the blood are. Such abilities are increasing as your community of scientists and thinkers move forward. They quantify the world of human knowledge in new ways. Why not join them by adding what we call knowing to the list. Be at that cutting edge as well.

Measure yourself soon. Look upon the flower and notice its magnificence. Look up at the tree and experience its presence. To what degree are you moved? Do you fall into love when you are with that flower, with that tree or patch of grass? Do you love that rock, the moisture in the air and the breeze at your cheek? Watch for that, the simple loving of life in each moment. Then watch where that feeling stops when you are thinking about politics. When you are appreciating a flower you are lifting yourself. You are also lifting your environment and all the world with that love. You are vibrating in truth. Increase your capacity to experience the richness of life.

The intelligence behind life as evidenced in your environment has always been and it will always be. The consciousness we are pointing you toward is that of eternity. It is intelligence upon intelligence, the ineffable, great joyous reality. A flower is evidence of it, and flowers come and go. Various environments are evidence of that intelligence, and those environments come and go. They always have and always will. This Earth is such an environment. It is evidence of the expression of the greatest heavens, but it also knows itself through the greatest hells. There are very poignant tragedies, real horrors of carelessness, apathy, disdain and hatred. Humans can display hatred to the maximum degree. They can heap malicious conduct on their fellows.

Ask yourself to access this fact, knowing that all of it is framed in the reality of its truth. And what is that truth? It is that which is real, which moves and lives and transforms. If it does not transform and it creates a hell in your body, then it is not truth with a capital "T," the Truth of your being, of your eternity. And how can you be one who expresses and lives in such Truth? You may offer kind gestures, give a blessing or smile in the sweetest way even to beings who may seem unworthy of it. The light of life shines on all. Why not be that kind of light?

As one attempting to live in truth, you might also be concerned and worried about unhelpful souls and unhelpful masters in both the Earth realm and in realms existing outside of the seen eye. Your human eyes mostly see only earthly beings. But some can see the other bodies that are in other dimensional realms. By coming here tonight, you have summoned certain masters. To most, Rhammah seems as one voice, but in energy Rhammah is many masters holding your attention with one voice. We take your minds on a journey of attention, delivering you to challenges. While that is happening you are being assisted, being held by high beings of light and love. They are a grand audience listening and speaking to you. Find a way inside yourself to say yes to the divine love that is being offered to every being here. Find a way to be with what seeps in, what is being whispering into the way you are wired.

For those who are able to see into the ethers, there are journeys, worlds upon worlds into multi-dimensional zones. Imagine what you are as a soul being like a castle with many rooms. Then become aware of the essence that flows through all of the castle's chambers. Divine intelligent life is everywhere, so measure yourself up next to what is presented and be with it without the commentary of a human. Be your truest self just humming along with the beauty of other dimensions. And don't despair if you have dreamed the most miraculous dreams and somehow there still are troubles. The genius that is life is exploring this collective experiment called humanity. The One, the Source before all sources is that essence which blows through every chamber of the great mansion that you are.

This is the essence that is dancing even in the hellacious tragedies of these days and your days. It is playing in the most corrupt politicians, in the most hated and the most hateful. And that same Source is in you, inhabiting your every cell and tissue. That is the one life and you are here to inhabit that truth, to a small degree and perhaps to a greater degree. You've arrived and this is the teaching. You might say, "Oh, Intelligence of the Universe, I know you are everywhere. And you are experimenting and you are playing in the world of politics, the world of business and in the world of daily life. Of course you are to inhabit all that is south of you, south of the highest heaven. Of course there are areas of our planet so dense that there seems to be no knowing of the harmony of life. And that which is life, that which you are has found a way to trick itself into the most twisted and difficult places."

As a human extension of this Supreme Intelligence, you also have difficult, twisted places in your own mind, in your own being and composition. Look honestly into those worlds within you. They are activated when you look at the news, when you see and feel sorrow for a tragedy in your world. This also exists as a room in the great mansion which is the life and essence of Source. As such, it plays and breathes through the halls and the many rooms of what you are. The balance we are speaking of is magnificent. For example, if you were a doctor in a war torn area, you could serve and represent that essence, healing the wretched and the saintly. In such a circumstance you could appreciate how life expresses itself in multitudes of ways.

We are highlighting in this example the mental attitude of a master of masters. The goodness of a saintly being should be measured against the cruelty in themselves. That saintly one realizes the mediocrity of their own self and thus can identify with those they serve. The latent tendencies of cruelty and hate, the saintly simply does not use those tendencies. Cruelty and hate inhabit a room of their being, but that room is simply not accessed. You may wonder how one attempts to live with this splitting up of spaces within. Understand that it is initially a mess to be a student of this teaching, initially. But think of the pioneers who took on great troubles to know a great adventure. There were certainly messes they made, but that did not stop them from exploring. They challenged the adventure and new situations evolved.

Those who sincerely seek an elevated spiritual point of view often have trouble with their family members, with their friends and even the world. Falling out of the slavery of humanity and deciding to live to the beat of your own drum can create social obstacles. Accept this part of finding a way to be with yourself that is real to you. Align with that which supports the wisdom you seek. There are two parts in this teaching. Be with life in the way that works for you, and then use the intelligence of that life as inspiration to face each day. To work at a coffee shop and deliver a muffin is God's work, so own it. If you are close to life and you feel the truth in it, there is nothing lesser about that. Live in the noble intent of each moment, and all you do will become an extension of what God does.

Very often when you ask for guidance, you are caught up in human notions of what success is. You want to be answered from those ideas about success which don't even work on this particular path towards wisdom. Why would we give you answers to such questions when eternity is the truth? Eternity is the truth and it is always with you. Simply love all that appears, for even the greatest human expressions have come and gone. Entire species have come and gone. We don't say this to encourage the greediness or reckless-ness of humans. No, we do not! We say this to reveal your misguided focus. We are highlighting the idea of just being with the flower, being without commentary so that you can discover love and vibrate in it. When you do that, humanity has just been touched through you and the whole world touches your very cheek, your whole self. Hold that moment and give it to yourself.

Give this new adventure your love and lean into it. Feel the warmth that is the possibility in your current shift and lean into that unknown. It is how the essence is delivered to you. Walking from one room into the next is all it is. Say yes to the tests, for they are growth. And get used to them, for they will not stop. Indeed, they will not stop. Most of your questions come from the basic difficul-ties of being human. Perhaps you were shortchanged an arm or a leg, a piece of your brain, whatever. Perhaps your parents were not kind and loving enough. Everyone has some difficulty or another. So, take a difficulty and use it. Be ennobled through it. Face your chal-lenge and work with it and stand for something.

To stand for something in a difficulty is to represent the intelli-gence of life. Life has created all of what is presented just as it is in every creature. You are life moving forward, striving. Say yes to that wisdom and fulfill your purpose. In your realm it is like everyone is a member of a great orchestra. There are those who play the triangle, the cello, the flute, the horn and so on. Some instruments have more prominent parts than others. Play your part in the divine dance and understand the equality of its wholeness. Everyone is part of the One, be they in the coffee shop, onstage, acting as a beggar or a helper to those needing service. Every part in life's dance is deserving of respect for its part in the great tapestry. There should be an equality of spirit within this oneness.

Think of your life as choices and consider how the realm of choices works. Underneath your world there are worlds of no choices, and above it there are ones with none as well. There are many worlds in the great system where there are no choices, there is just the path of harmony, the way of the heavens. It is grace upon grace upon grace, purity at work and everything is beautiful and delightful. Below this world there is so much density. There are places of no movement and no choice. For some who move out of those hells into this one, even the opportunity to experience choice through cruelty and meanness is an awesome freedom. Beings who choose to experience this world in those ways are sometimes sent right back. They are sent back to the black tar of choicelessness which indeed can seem like they are there forever and forever.

(A participant asks, "Who sends them back and why?") They go back as a result of their own compilation of choices. They are pulled by the gravity of their own energy. There is the very messy quality of teaching humans what is true. That is what we are dealing with here. You are given results based on what you are choosing. This fact can sometimes be altered depending on what your circumstances have been. In practical terms as a human you have choice and culpability. But in some situations you almost have no choice by merit of your ignorance. For example, a human may choose to steal when the occasion presents itself because all that one has known were selfish people who did the same with impunity. That is a choice in one way, but not in another. They are in the gravity of both the soul family and the blood family. You are all in types of gravity having inherited a set of circumstances. The realm of choice, in practical terms, is what you must use to move into the good gifts of life, into the better worlds. There are those who are given the choice between prison and gang life. Which is better? They have

109

inherited that and it is all they know. Do you feel sorry for them? Their gravity caused that.

(*Participant asks, "How do they go beyond that. How do they change and get out of the density?"*) Within the context of gang life and prison life you make tough uphill choices. You can move out of the pull of your sisters and brothers and their tribal mindsets. Then if one makes many little courageous choices they may inherit a new reality in weeks, months, years or lifetimes. It is a context, a teaching that is often necessary. One who sits in prison can contemplate these worlds and arrive to the higher understandings. They can discover the Lord of Their Being by resting. Occasionally they can instantly bust through many worlds and many karmas. Then it may seem like they won the lottery. Their life is new and it looks like they have completely changed. They inherit gifts and a whole new set of circumstances. So, if perchance you are in such difficulties, know that it is a great way to quicken your desire for wisdom.

For the aspirant who wants to receive knowing from the God of Their Being, they must wrestle with paradoxes on every level. How this works is not fully able to be grasped by the limited mental capacity of human experience. You can serve certain people and then grow into this world. Find a way to teach with a certain type of consciousness. Why does the framework of good and evil become so necessary to grasp? Upon direct observation there are actually various degrees of ignorance which you might label as evil. Qualities of density and ignorance can intensify and get heavier, but they can also lighten up. On the highest level it is all just the universe dancing. It dances in density, in lightness and in complexity, always exploring. In the lowest of the low and the highest of the high, in all expressions within each realm there are those who seek creativity. They can seek it through their anger, in their pride and in their egos.

Each being seeks to play and express various qualities within themselves. Every realm has its creators and its innovators. Inside of you are these complex and very tempting shadowy forces pulling on you. And then there are the more noble aspects of yourself manifesting. In the realm of choice, point your attention towards being noble. A class could be taught on that with very powerful effects. In the biggest picture there is the Source of All expressing a reflection of its higher virtues in contrast to its lower virtues. In essence it is all just light and shadow on the surface of a pond. In your sense of being separate human persons, are you going to get lost in the colors and the qualities? Or are you going to watch it from the distance? It's up to you. (*Participant says, "Thank you, thank you for answering my questions."*)

There are some hurting heads in the room. (*Chuckles from group.*) We feel it when we give answers like yes and no, this or that. Let's try to put the questions you are asking on various levels into context. The answers you want come from a place of incompleteness within you. The answers we give intend to assist you on a quest for discovering wholeness. There is a skill in choosing an inquiry. It is defined by how you shape your mind. You can ask to know in a way that would have your whole nature disappear into beauty as it unleashes through you. That beauty moves into function. It is inspiration expressed in love and built upon love.

Such beauty inhabits the everywhereness of life and you become porous by embracing it. It teaches you to sit with your whole being and ask yourself questions that get you to your wholeness. Asking such questions should eventually take apart the urge to ask questions. What is thinking and what would it mean if thinking fell apart? What if that happened and all you had was the beloved quality of grace and beauty? How far away from this teaching are you? We have given you tools to measure it with. Do whatever you need to. Sit by a river. Look at the image of a lake. Look at a piece of art. Watch your breath. Look upon your friends, those you love and ask yourself if you are experiencing delight and love.

While doing this, notice if your mind is trying to make it right because your mind thinks something is wrong. Perhaps your mind says, "Why doesn't the world see the beauty in this flower like I do?" We would reply, "Why are you not seeing that beauty right now when thinking of the world?" The wisdom we share reminds you to vibrate with the intelligence that made the flower. Do it in such a way that the world is new to you. That is how you change your life from the inside out. That is the quality of seeing how this works on the inside and using it in your life. Such a movement into love requires seeing all the manifest qualities anew. And that should be the movement of your life. Life itself changes because you are seeing it from the standpoint of eternity, as eternity.

This is how creative energy works in oneness with the intelligence that created everything. And that Intelligent Source will always be here. It cannot be destroyed. It cannot ever be destroyed. If you are in this knowing, living is effortless. What's called for is immediately acknowledged in vibration by your essence as, "Of course it is right that I act in accordance with this truth." Find a way to be with the energy which the masters are bringing. See the synchronicity of your life. Hear what the birds and animals are saying in various circumstances. It is a gift that not everybody naturally has, but all of you can develop it to one degree or another. And that capacity becomes even clearer when you move beyond thinking that it is so special to have that capacity.

Be completely mind to mind with life. Pick something like the hardness of the floor, the softness of a feather or the colors in your environment and let them be mind to mind, heart to heart, belly to belly and bone to bone. Inhabit this moment with your whole self as vibration being with vibration. Energy is everywhere and this knowing is in you, vibrate with it. Be mind to mind with your fellows, with the masters who are here all about you. Have resolve for this kind of truth. Take the qualities of wisdom derived from your struggle, from what you've inherited and sit with them. Take the highest and most noble awareness in your dedicated life and grow with that.

So dear students, practice embracing the life you chose, the one you would love. Tune up how you focus that. Get this and get to the essence of the vision so that you are sure it represents the highest in you. For upon their death bed, no soul wishes they had twenty mansions and thirty Rolls Royce's. There are, however, many souls who wish they had greater abundance or more connections. Many wish to have known the depths of friendship. But no soul says, "The popularity I fought for all my life will sustain me." No soul says that. The qualities of your connections is what you can take with you.

How do you create greater focus? Ask yourself new questions about what you would have for yourself. Create your life differently, so that when you think of yourself on a beach and feel the breeze, when you are in the abundance of that manifestation, you bring this level of emotional energy into it. Emote the completeness and fullness of that vision. Sit in oneness with it. When all that exists is in that elevated vibration, it is all just life. So our second teaching is this. There is only fullness whether you live under a bridge or in a mansion, whether you have a thousand friends or none.

Resolve to find the balance that exists within these teachings. For example, your life does matter and also in eternity, your life is but on a grain of sand. Practice this bigness and then get inside that grain of sand and inhabit it with magnificence. Put on your human suit and own it. Get the job at the coffee shop and pour that coffee with love. Be that divinity in action, so complete and whole. What you can take with you when you leave this world is that integrity. The quality of abundance you feel when you abide with your fellow humans is a grace you own in reverence. Rhammah is of you, indeed. There is only God and also there is God expressing itself in multitudes.

You are in relationships with your brothers and your sisters, your immediate family, your community and all of humanity. You are also in community with the endless number of souls in all worlds, those who have passed through this world and moved on from it. Rhammah is a system of masters expressing itself through a Host while also sitting next to you whispering in your ear. We holding you up in the vibration of Love. Rhammah is everything and everywhere, just as you are everything and everywhere. And you are also a character in this dream, pursuing function and purpose and the breakthrough of the next day. What an adventure. Get on board.

What can you do when all of these things are true? Anything and nothing. What is true when all of these things are true? Everything and nothing. Everything and nothing is true, while at the same time you can be completely focused on discerning truth. It is a paradox that is difficult for you to fully grasp. So, discern deliberately by asking the Lord of Your Being to inhabit this moment and to inhabit your life. Have radical perspective. If you are not on this trip in some way, through some methodology, you are missing out on the greatest adventure ever. It is a challenge for you to be all that you are completely. Why would you take on any other challenge before this one? Why would you come to receive this wisdom and not act on it in some way, not live with it on some level? You will be loved no matter what, even if you don't use these teachings. Do you wonder if I am selling you something? What if I could sell you to yourself like a being who could sell ice to an Eskimo or water to a fish?

What else is there really but to know the ultimate truth? What you come here asking for, in essence is so incredibly close. Just by moving out of the way, reflections of self and truth occur. So point yourself towards Eternity. Be this truth. Rhammah is so impressed to see you all here. These are challenging teachings. Bless you if you come back. Bless you if you don't. Bless you. I am you, you are I

114

and you are loved. That is so right and so true. You are infinite love and I am that also. The great sea of energy is in every drop of your being. Affirm that now. Live that truth now and in these days that are ahead. Rhammah bids thee adieu. I am so impressed.

ETERNITY

Look inside and give it all up

Trust the directive to be here

Join the richness of truth

Ride on the seas of divine intention

Trust that it is here, on the other side of giving up

There is nothing in the way

Acknowledge you are this great eternity

Discourse 2: Say Yes to the Eternal Source

You are reading this because you have a desire to know an uplifted reality or have studied an uplifting reality and are on a quest to sing of that in the material world. There are others like you, and you flock with each other around a higher vibration and concepts that lift you out of heavy thinking. In your world, thinking has more gravity. It is more pedestrian and it moves slower. Rhammah comes in from an infinite reality and has to slow itself down in an attempt to match up with your world. On the other layers of reality, in the other worlds instant knowingness is always present. In those realms conversations with your fellows are done spontaneously, simultaneously, with individual knowingness directly connected to the knowingness of All. Thoughts are not separated and the information manifests at God's speed. It is instant, so quick that it cannot be measured as time for it is without time.

There is a very cumbersome agreement here on Earth, for you have taken on a human vessel in a material reality. Here it all seems so incredibly real as you lift your body and move it to get it places. You have to take care of it in a very pedestrian way. You work, hunt, do whatever it takes to bring nourishment to the vessel, to house it and take care of it. And how is your relationship to all of that going? It can often feel burdensome, for your birthright, your legacy is of the infinite which is divine. Do you present in and relate to this world like an ambassador from another country? Indeed, that is what you are. You are a forever being visiting this world and you have forgotten that basic fact. You are lost in being humanly identified, often not taking care of what your potential can be for the world and for others. Do you agree that divinity is in you? Will you agree to discover that and present it in your daily lives? Is your practice to take care of your household, your body, your food and your families in the noblest way possible? It takes earnest effort to live that life.

It is possible to find a way to establish a correct relationship within the limitations of family members. The core question is, can you be in the world as who you really are? And, are you willing to do what it takes for another inch of that to be true in whatever way? Be more of yourself today and take care of yourselves. Be more present with your household. This is not just a logical teaching. Its backdrop is the fact that you are great and magnificent eternal beings, here for a limited time. Graduation arrives in this world with the recognition of those qualities. The full understanding of this is finally being presented. When this happens a new destiny manifests. Your destiny as an eternal being has manifested in this realm. It has landed, made its mark and now you can graduate. You can move on.

Contemplate how you can align with that mark. Consistently ask yourself about the need to study the whole world's wisdom in such a way that it makes sense to your life. You can adjust to include that and become authentic in your interactions. Yes, there is work to do, for the personality is often entangled in troubles. Do whatever it takes to undo entanglements so that effortless knowing of the spiritual reality can blossom. Tend to yourself and your relationships. You need to do that so the greater, effortless grace can function more completely here in this world. Do you desire to do this? Do you want to make way for the potential to be not just a human being, but a spiritual being? Strive to establish a way of functioning that is graceful, kind, straight and impassable.

There are so many ways that this can manifest because each person has a set of relative realities. But there is one thing that is not relative, and that is honestly maturing into the circumstances you are in. Ask for that and cooperate with a way that brings about the capacity for your spiritual nature to be fully born here. For some it means great service, working the food kitchen, helping the homeless or being of service to your friend. To others it means creating works of art, enriching oneself in the depths of intuition. And in some it needs to be about a sense of worship, realizing reality in others and in yourself. Find your way to represent the connectedness of yourself and others authentically, for you are all in the same boat.

A shift in attitude like the one we are proposing goes into every emotional impulse in your body. It affects every subtle reality in your being. It travels into thought, which is also of energy. This is a part of how vibration works, and that vibration helps or hinders your fellows. It increases in power when a network of beings shares such an endeavor, trying to become more aligned with their spiritual nature. You are affecting and you are being affected by that collective of eternal divine beings. These virtual gods are more than what you think on a practical and immediate level. You are also far more than you could ever imagine. Access this collective and you access an amazing intelligence with power that is beyond you. In truth, you are all a part of a certain destiny and you are tied together in that. You are an evolving soul and there is an inarguable gravity in the movement of such souls. It asks you to make choices based on the inarguable directive of collective thought and of your environment.

In this, there is a higher calling. Your sense of autonomy is an illusion within this greater reality. And a very complex and brilliant design is at work which you are integrally connected to and intimately interlocked with. When you look into your being and see it from the soul level, your choice is either yes to evolution or no. And, there is a natural way to act in soul evolution. If you are not taking care of your body and mind, or if you are encumbered with duress and drama, you will not be in contact with this natural way. The farther you go on this path, the more you realize there is no choice. You will simply know that this is what I'm supposed to do and this is just going to happen. No more is needed. It is okay to access things through rational processes, but it is no longer needed.

At some level you will know what is called for in the design of these circumstances. It is no longer about you, but rather about the energies of the universe at work. Be quiet enough to detect the way these winds need to blow. And don't lose track of your soul's directive which took on this body and this life. It has a specific mission which may run counter to the whims of fellows and kin. It urges and directs you through inner truth. To be sucked into the milieu of conditioning is not being spiritual. Going with the flow at a fancy drug party is not spiritual. And, saying yes in a literal way to such enterprises is not what we are speaking about. We speak about an eternal yes to reality and the fact that your life has manifested in the way it needs to. In this flow you will take on the tough decisions because of the true knowing in the core of your being.

By reading these words, you are allowing us to massage you with these various truths, and our hands are very large, very loving and very kind. We are here, behind your thoughts and are present with you caring in the way that the masters care. Masters care in a way similar to how many parents see their children. We are like parents who have been through it all and see the greater truths. So we pay attention to those greater truths that are not easy for you to comprehend. These truths have a higher vibration and an energetic quality that uplifts you into those realities. Get used to it. Contact your body energy, your aura and give it over to the sacred. Turn it over to the Beloved Divine and the higher will of the Universe. Get used to it. Look inside and give it all up. Trust the directive you've been called here to be a part of. Join the richness of that truth.

There is a vibrational heaven and a way of experiencing it that is abundant, joyous and full of vitality. Trust that it is there on the other side of you giving up the need to figure it out, the need to have a rational process for your life. In this vibration every room of your being becomes an open place where the winds of your divine nature blow through, animate and enliven. In this enlivened state, allow your greater nature to take the whole mansion onto the seas of divine intention. Do you have a sense of how many rooms you have? There are closets and cubby holes. There are spaces in the rafters, the attic, the cellar and the many corners of the whole dwelling from foundation to roof. You can turn it all over to the higher will. Give it up to the one wind that blows through. In doing so you are aligning and acknowledging that you are eternity. That eternity can express itself completely, for there is nothing in the way.

This mansion of yours is composed of the various things you have figured out for yourself on the rational level. Those strategies may seem to work for a time and then they don't. They are your best guesses in any situation. In heavy conditioning they are the places in you that need to have it a certain way. You fixate on these positions because you identify with past experience as a source of truth. But past experience becomes wisdom when you turn it over to eternity. Then you can use the experience and the various qualities of a lifetime brilliantly. You no longer have to figure it out. So, be transfigured into this way of relating that is dynamic, alive and exhilarating. There is no fear when this is your reality because all of the pockets of your mind, all of the interdimensional worlds and dream worlds are turned over to the great eternal truth. Energetically and in all of the worlds which culminate through the great journey of your soul, you are turned over to the Great Eternity, the One Source.

Choose to allow that wind to blow through and animate your life. Choose to be that great eternal truth while scrubbing the floor, organizing the house, analyzing data, fixing machinery and facing the reality of your day. Do this with strength, nobility, kindness and the capacity to relate effectively and gently without attitude. Let it evolve, creating beautiful potentials. Insist that your homes represent creative magnificence from bottom to top. This represents your decision to be of that Source that you came from and that you are. The balance is natural, for your foundation and that which assists you in functioning is not separate from what you do. Be an inspiring, brilliant philosopher, a highly effective carpenter, office person, ditch digger, mother, whatever. It matters not what you do if it is done in this alignment.

Your life is a spiritual practice that becomes effortless when you allow yourself to know about that One Source. This grandness is the very core of your being. Discover it as a magnificent, intelligent wind that turns you on. It bears fruit that you cannot imagine. It needs to be discovered more than taught. The masters who have found it can tell you it is possible, worth it, and that you can do it. Perhaps it is time for another inch, and then another inch ten years later. Incrementally probe farther into the truth of your being. Armed with this wisdom, you are in the right situation to internally accelerate your awakening process. Rhammah will assist you. Our invisible hands are of eternity, each cell, each atom is alive with that One Source. So, say yes to the great riches of the One Source. Say yes to the very core of your being and to your reason for becoming incarnate in the first place eons ago. All of the journeys you have been on, all of the worlds that are in you are being acknowledged as that One Source.

Find a way to use your gifts and enter your life awake to the unique qualities that are appearing. The gifts of your being will be fully utilized as the One Source animates you and shows you a dynamic potential. Evolve masters, evolve, evolve, evolve. Immense knowing and power is immediately available when you say yes from the core of your being, to that which is at the core of your being. Say yes, with every atom in your body. From the Source that created each atom make a choice to say yes. You are a great miracle and the energies of awakening pour around the periphery of your being.

Attune them to your life. Be kind and gentle to yourself and to the environment you are in.

Understand that you have many rooms which you visit, and these rooms often have difficulty talking with one another. The One Source will assist an instantaneous relating between the many rooms, between the many worlds and yourself. You will be able to simplify the way you present yourself. Imagine that you can pull your energies together into a bundle and focus them. The God of your Being says yes to coming forth and functioning as one power. So, when you pull yourself together, you are pulling together a vast wonderful self and focusing it into the moment in a highly effective manner. Appreciate your vastness and the beauty that you give others. For the life you are living is completely magnificent and inspiring. Continue to let others nurture you towards this.

Each atom in your being is alive with the power of Source. That Source in you has no end and its power is without end. Say yes with more and more of your being. Simply say yes to the Everything. Accelerate this dance with your eternity, with more moments of your day, more movements in a year as you journey towards this knowing. Align to that now in the depths of your being for your lives are about that destiny. By saying yes to a higher vibration you are serving humanity and showing the world the way to an integrated destiny. Your determination to move past your neurosis, to become more courageous, to serve your family in greater peace and to serve others is an inspiration that uplifts the world.

What's at work here is far greater than you. It is being inspired by Allness. It inspires you to say, "On the behalf of all I live this life. I choose this endeavor for the love of all of life. I choose it and do it with integrity." Rhammah bids thee adieu. We are all very impressed.

INFINITE LOVE

Fall into infinite love

Disappear into infinite love

Rest into infinite love

Drop into infinite love

Relax into the sacred grace of infinite love

Discourse 3: Relate as the Infinite with All that Unfolds

There is infinite wisdom, and how all is seen from infinite wisdom. Rhammah has an advantage knowing how it looks from the vastness. The power that you wish for through your methods and your strategies is accessed most easily from that viewpoint. The Infinite is simply being itself and it is natural to be with that pure power, that pure being. All that you are as seeing, hearing, touching, tasting, and smelling is the overflow of Infinite Being. It is its gesture, for Infinite Being is inclined to play in diversity, in the softness of a feather, the hardness of a rock or in the crystal clarity of a diamond. It will play and play in the many colors, for the Infinite manifests. Rest into that greatness. Like a baby would pick up a toy, imagine you are the Infinite picking up this realm, knowing what you yield has presence.

Bringing that forth is natural if you can pinch off your capacity for unrest. In the feverish grasping, the helping and in your concerned nature there is the sense that the greater capacity of your concerns are unacknowledged. And so, your questions come from that concerned nature. Great masters, for you to really be of service to yourselves and to your friends, look at the fever you are all in. Losing your house or going broke are easy expressions if you know the Infinite. Suppose you are homeless, jobless, penniless, hungry and cold. Those are all natural gestures of the Infinite. Welcome your new adventure, for it will pass. From the Infinite perspective these are just comings and goings.

The greatest capacity to relax into power is to know gentleness, for gentleness comes from how the naturalness of creation works. This may seem contrary to human perception, but you can actually know how gentle it is that meteors pass through space at great speeds and collide. This comes from the relaxed power that is gravity. It is just power overflowing in all of its destructiveness and awesomeness, in all of its infinite gentility like the softness of a feather. Complex organisms come forth in the great garden that is your planet. They also come from that natural easiness. And you can adjust your energy to resonate with that.

There are many wise teachings on your planet that embody this fact. They offer a way to gently be with your pain, with your knotted distress. They allow you to gently be with what unfolds as the adventure, the hero's journey and with the new dream of knowing which forms from the dying of that adventure. This new dream comes from the Infinite. Humans are caught up in their hurriedness to heal, to care as if the sky is falling or that a fire is afoot. They act like there is something wrong. You as a healer can raise your hand to the sky in the gentle, natural power of blessing. You might say, "Enough, enough, slow down and be with this perceived problem, for energy is everywhere. You are a great healing vibration, and all that passes is limited. You have blessed others with your presence, with your light and your adventure."

A list of observations come from this ultimate cache of reference. The whole adventure is placed perfectly, even as you doubt it, even as your mind is looking for rhyme, or reason, or why. The natural inclination of the Infinite knows that there is no loss and there is no gain, there is just the ongoing dance. So go forth and give yourself to an adventure. Play like a Michelangelo with a stone. Having schooled yourself for weeks on how to take a machine across the road, take a vehicle to the far coast and come back. Then the adventure is done just like you are born a human only to die. This is the natural inclination of the Infinite. To create universes only so they will collapse, this is what infinity does. And it does it in infinite love, although you struggle with that truth.

So the way you relate to "that which unfolds," is an undergoing transformation. It is a cosmic way of being with so much power, full of knowing. The Infinite is its quantum self as an unfed, dirty beggar. That is a quantum, worthy adventure, a natural gesture of an overflowing Infinity. The whole universe is Cosmic Being expressing itself in multitudes of adventures. The way things unfold may be different than you expect, so learn to adjust. You also can simply arrive to call forth the infinite knowing within you and yield to its truth. You are each planters of seeds, asking questions. So, how do you plant seeds of wisdom? You watch for an opening when the right question is asked and then you share.

So share in a relaxed state, delighted to be with others and to be of great use on the planet. A natural gesture of the infinite overflowed in itself to such a degree that you were born. Behold, behold how this is so true, even as you criticize your dance and what plays out in your life. The wrestling and fighting you bring to yourself is because you shortchanged yourself. Try easing up so that this greater nature can flourish and play forth through your vessel, through the organism that receives these words. For an energetic network exists around your cranium with feelers that receive. It is all a way for the overflowing of Infinity to play through into this dimension, a way for Infinity as you to play forth.

The network that is a soul with memories moving through it, is that all you are? The answer is that you are the infinity that came forth, that poured forth of itself to play in diversity. All that is beheld is beheld by you, and so therefore it is in you. When you are dreaming, the whole of the dream and all of the characters, are they not also of you? As your eyes awaken from one dream, here you are in another dream. That distant mountain is inside of your being and its beauty thunders in your soul. The resonance in your dimension is proof of that fact, for when you are moved by beauty energy pulses through you. This is the evidence that what you are viewing is in you. It is of you and ultimately from you. What beauty you have given to this character in the center of a great dream on this planet you call Earth.

You are that glorious infinite one playing. Dump your concerns for this moment and for as many moments as you can, and just rest in this truth. You are full of the intuitive juice that is life. That is what heals. So let this vast gentleness play through that which is playing out through words, deeds, gifts and reflections. Do that on every level. Quietly sit with your friend holding this concept in your mind. Just doing that embodies the Infinite on their behalf. And when you know of the power which is natural to that fact, you will never again worry whether you are pushing enough energy, giving enough or being enough. For when you relax and sit with your friends, you are offering the naturalness of your infinity, the gentle power that has no end.

When you see the mountain it is evidence of your creation, of the power emoted by you. When you contact the knowing, there is a cognition that the mountain needs to be no different than as it is. For it is the quiet voice of infinite power. The bum who is sleeping under the stone bench needs not be any different than the way he or she is. That one is resting into that which is creating all. Grasp this truth as you look squarely at the hungry little critter in an organism called you. You, the one who wants to run away with impulses, hurriedness and human concerns, that you is not resting in the mastery of knowing what is possible. Surviving should not even be a concern for a knowing, infinite being. Dancing in the experience of the moment with full awareness should be the focus.

So what of Rhammah? What is that to you humans? Rhammah is a name given to you for what? A voice speaks through a human vessel and gives you the name Rhammah. But what goes with that voice, something that coagulates everywhere and yet nowhere? It is not of a substance like you know yourselves to be. All of the images and gestures that appear to your mind, the face of the Host, that is not Rhammah. All of the impressions, all of the individuality that you might tag onto Rhammah, is not Rhammah. Even in the inclination to share what Rhammah is, understand that what I am is not that either. What of my visits through other vessels in days past? Indeed, it has been done before under different names, because Rhammah is just a name for the love that is everywhere. In reality I am you. This voice, these words in your awareness are of your being, of your dream. It is your creation that is simply going big, answering you on the level that matters as you live on the crest which overflows through Infinite Being.

We give you these poetic words to shock your mind out of the place where your questions come from. Not that questioning isn't good, but there is so much more. You can rest and relax into all that you are. If you can't see the clock, you may have doubts about the ticking. The same is true about bodies breathing if you can't see them. The breathing of your neighbor becomes disassociated and you experience the directness of sitting with what is appearing empty of associations. Being in that state is a great blessing for your body and for others. So, as your eyes are closed, feel the sensations that are of the body and its energetic qualities. But what do they mean if you forget the association with body, if you are empty of the images of body? You may find a change in your habit of comparing, contrasting and of assigning labels. Sensory reality that is empty of associations can cause boundaries to dissolve. There can be an easing up or a call to speak into the infinite blessedness. Relax towards that sacred grace. Disappear into it and all will be handled exquisitely.

Forget the chatter and speak into this depth. It is okay and it is completely safe to disappear into the vast infinite love. Let the mind's voice come from the belly of your being and speak into the silence as you rest. It is completely okay to rest into the infinite love, realizing that all there is, is infinite love. Let your questions float into this heavenly knowingness that is essence itself. It is okay to be the infinite pool in such a way that all there is, is infinite love. Sense that your struggle to feel safe can be given to that palpable, never ending pool. You can give this alignment as a salve to your grasping and learn to feel safe away from the pool of energy. Give this away, in such a way as you are always infinite love. It is a giving up until there is only infinite love. Drop into the infinite, fall, rest, let all of the knowledge you've gathered spin away and whirl into the energy. Give it up to the vast power that is infinite love, that which you are.

In this infinite love there is a carefree state where the seeking for answers dismantles. You will experience a dropping, a resting into what you truly are. If there is any question of whether or not you are doing this exercise correctly, whether or not you are following Rhammah's teachings correctly, watch where that is coming from. The one who wants to be free, the one who wants to be bettered or upgraded can be sat with. They can be included in such a way that there is a dismantling of comparative concepts. Even to delight in this teaching or be elated that you are here, that whole construct can be given up for it all just is. The subtlest urgency coming from the human disposition can be sat with lovingly and can be included in the pool of energy so that all there is, is this. Even the slight, smallest evidence of your personal identity can be absorbed into this infinite oneness, every image, every dream. It can be done.

It is alive and true that questions, and ways of being, and the asking of services comes from the human struggling. That struggling creates a disharmony in the body. The aching comes from being lost in the dream. Your job is to relate as the infinite with all that unfolds and not spend your resources unwisely. For indeed, this truth that is of you, it is powerful. It does not validate human urges. In fact, it is a threat to them. They are in danger of being dissolved. However, honoring the timeliness of the universe is a gentle endeavor. And sharing gently, when and where there is a true opening, that is what you are employed for by taking on this teaching. Your evolution happens in response to your revelations. It is propelled forward by your earnestness to be in the mystery of this truth. You are pulling it in. Rhammah will always be with you for I am in you, I am of you, and this has always been true. (*a long, silent pause.*)

We watch you energetically when you are given silence. Your mind says, "What do I do with this empty moment?" There is an uh-oh that comes up. The uh-oh is an opportunity to look at how you are relating. Spend time in front of a blank page or empty canvas. Establish yourself as creator and honor that. There is so much grandeur and aliveness in your capacity to lay down a color in any way you feel like in the moment. It can also go into a phone call with your friend. You sit with that phone like a blank canvas. It is exquisite to share, to give words with knowing. Let it be the overflow of the Infinite. Do not give yourselves less than this. Do not shortchange your power. To wonder what Rhammah would say is shortchanging yourself. Say what you know.

Understand that the artwork is yours, as is the overflow of the Infinite. By completely surrendering to the owning of this, there is no right or wrong way of doing. There is just the beloved power that picks up that form and is with all of creation. It is your human job to stay out of its way. For us, linking to your minds is quite entertaining. (*group laughter*) The soup of myths and histories and assumptions, there are so many little ingredients. Let them be in the energy. Let none of them be wrong. But also just let them be, for indeed they are. As you practice this lesson, you are simply resonating with the fact that everything is of that infinite love energy. This is for now a complete teaching. We bid you adieu.

ARE YOU CALLING?

Are you making a call?

Are you asking for a sense of direction into the mystery?

Are you yearning for wisdom?

Rhammah is answering
Rhammah comes to us, out of service
Rhammah comes to us as a cluster of energies
Rhammah comes to us realized and alive with truth

So rest….Be still.....Know you are loved

Discourse 4: Beyond the Gravity of "Me Identity"

In the ocean of love there are many fish, many beings who live there. Many beings are set up to come into a vessel and live a lifetime. I am Rhammah and I am set up to come into a vessel lived by another. I come for a brief moment in time out of service to you as you yearn for wisdom. Whether you know it or not, you are making a phone call. You are calling upon a calling, asking for a sense of direction into the mystery. Rhammah is a cluster of energies, a cluster of intelligent masters realized and alive with truth. Many of you may be comforted as you watch words being ushered from this voice, as you hear teachings and see awesome gestures produced. Of course, for the Host it is still a strange trip to be kicked out of his body so an entity can use it for a moment.

Know that as you sit here you are being taught energetically. So rest, be still and know that you are loved. Know you are being taught mind to mind by masters who sit next to you and all around you holding you lovingly. They press you with the meaning behind these words and reveal worlds of knowing that are available to you. Here you may glimpse the awesome ultimate knowing of yourself as the very boundless, infinite reality of love. This boundless reality of love can exist in the human imagination as you train the mind to affirm it forever. The rest is doing it and achieving a physiological balance.

In discovering spiritual reality, you are discovering the great ocean. And all the fish of the ocean are also of its waters and all its elements. Or you may think of it like a cake made up of ingredients. You are creatures made up of ingredients of various worlds. You think back on gods and myths about all of these energies that are stirred in to make you. A tablespoon of salt may be a tablespoon of

Zeus, or a tablespoon of Brahma or Yahweh. You might also say it's random, abstractly made of this and that.

Such reflections depersonalize your structure as a being and ask you to rest in the greater, grander nature that is of forever. Would you dare do this? There is actually great resistance in all of you towards the idea of disappearing into the loving light of forever. You have this resistance even as forever calls you and shows you that there is so much peace available. You realize there is this forever, but you say, "I want to be a me, and I want to have my cake also." And the tricky thing is there is nothing wrong with cake. There is nothing wrong with any experience in humanity. And there is nothing wrong with any experience in consciousness. But there are stakes of energy, stakes of awareness that you may come to discover.

All of these are reflections on the many ways Infinite Love dances and plays. It even plays as suffering and destruction. There is the glorious light, but the shadow is also there. Every drop of water dances collectively in the pond. It is like that in the whole play of human experience, the joyous and the hellacious in all of the dimensions. As complex and magnificent as it is, it is all one energy dancing in many ways. It bedazzles you and creates scenarios for you to get lost in. Storylines are kept alive and their velocity is made possible by your grasping onto the "me identity." Those who aspire to have freedom must move out of the pull, out of the orbit of that "me consciousness."

It often takes great effort. It is advisable to be open to guidance on what type of effort to use and how the effort should be applied. Each student brings a set of conditions. You are students of this work, taking on encouragement and assistance from your fellows and from the teachings as you study and apply them. You can use tried and true wisdoms as you intend to move past the "me identity" and move out of the orbit of the noisy mind. How this is approached can be done differently in various schools of thought. It is important to be awake in all methods. It is advised to be dedicated, consistent and tenacious about moving out of the orbit of me. It takes a lot of fuel to get a ship out of your atmosphere and gravity. But once in orbit, a satellite around your planet does not need endless amounts of rocket fuel. Once in orbit, a small pulse can make that ship move through miles and miles of space.

The discovery of the Lord of Your Being and relaxing into it can be thought of like putting yourself in that space that is beyond the gravity of "me identity." You are resting in the orbit of your eternal truth. How consciously can you do that? How repetitively can you override the heavy efforts that the human heart brings to the task of awakening? Can you measure up to the sensibilities of an awakened being? There are many ways to try. You can chant a mantra and pray for awakening. You can listen to the words of a master and move into the master's orbit. And there is listening and allowing the self to go gentler and gentler into the great orbit of knowing yourself as infinite love, as divinity itself. We have put our heart up to the energy that is here, and we lead the palpable directive of this collective which is an expression of The One Source. Each person who partakes of this wisdom is potentially an awesome force. For you have insight on how to be a causal agent in your realm, and in yourself.

Move into an intimacy with your own mind, your own field as you sense the communication with energy. Match up with the blessings that are being offered to you through this wisdom. Allow your body, mind, brain and thinking to be adjusted so it fits in with this higher energy. Allow and surrender to it. There are those of you who make the effort to speak naturally from your heart. You let others know how you actually get lost, how the human dance goes for you. Doing this loosens the prose. It loosens your being and lets people in. Everyone has sadness, anger and fear, and it is all okay. You can love the mind/body which the human inhabits and allow it to be touched by divinity,allowing it to be what it is. You often get hot and bothered, agitated or sorrowful and that's okay. Be natural about being human.

With that said, you are all doing perfectly fine and there is nothing wrong. But at the same time there is the urgency in you to discover your potential. And there is no greater potential than viewing others as real humans in the real struggle. It is a heartfelt awakening to speak of how your knees shake, how your self-consciousness works, how your bitterness and your vulnerability work. You let others in by sharing your efforts in dealing with such human realities while attempting to remembering your higher associations to Oneness. Put this teaching right in front of you. Devour it and make your effort. For when you start, you can get a sense of how your human emotional energy and the walk into spiritual energy can be emoted, held up, integrated and moved forward.

To live in service to others as a spiritual being is so uplifting. In order to do that authentically you have to be an example, fighting through your "me identity" in an effort to uplift. Relating to others authentically helps you match up in vibration with others. It helps you do it with humility. For example, you might say, "Like you, I am moving into this, struggling to shift my understanding of what I really am. Still to this day my knees shake and I walk forward anyway. The human part of me is alive and kicking, but the spiritual part also wins many times a day." That is authentic. The strident and free spiritual self, the magnificent embodiment of divinity and love that you are needs to be invited into your consciousness even as you walk forward like a wobbly, vulnerable human. You have to hang open like a kite in the wind saying, "Here I am, warts and all, knobby knees, whatever." Allow yourself to be seen transparently.

It is essential to be an authentic human first, to love the human part of you completely. Take care of it and to speak for it. All of the gods are guiding the human vehicle no matter if it is an old man, an aunt or an uncle, a child, a hero or even a committee. It is complex, mysterious and more often than not it is one heck of a mess. And embracing that messiness, being honest sets you up to receive guidance through the winds of truth. There is nothing more beautiful for a human being than to be thrown into service mode. There are those of you who are healers and are being asked by your circumstances to sit with those who suffer. The greatest dances come from the depths of living through an ordeal. And those depths are better contacted by relating with your humanness and allowing a greater energy to pour through the human vehicle.

You might say to one who is suffering, "I can try to understand you. I know I can't fully do that, but I can be with you through this. I have my own struggles, so I have a way to relate to what you are going through. And I know of the value of having a steadfast presence in my life. I have craved it from childhood until this day. So, I will attempt to be that for you. I will be infinite love for you, steadfast, clear and resolved. I will hold elevated vibrations as you dance with your mortality, your dilemma, your illness, and all that you go through. Let's look into it together. Let's both be honest."

The winds of freedom are everlasting, awesome and divine. They are there for those who are living beyond themselves. So if it takes hours of meditation to deliver yourself beyond yourself, do it. If it takes service and charity work, do it. It may take re-prompting many times a day with moments of pause and self-talk. This teaching is about being available to the winds of infinite love. For a contracted human who is lost, suckling upon its thumb, curled in upon itself often needs help. There is nothing wrong with that. That individual who is helped, when they find their way will see the light. They will realize that seeing past self is the way. So, the key to relieving suffering is watching how "the me" dances cleverly all the time in subtle and profound ways. It creates assumptions that one is assailed by unjust forces. It creates ways to be wobbly and less capable.

Those who study this wisdom know that what is available is a lifted consciousness. You know that you do not have to be defined by your circumstances. A shift, a reorientation is possible. On this path, at times you may fall into the outer reaches of "the orbit of me" where the gravity of individual focus is lessened. Be effortlessly there and allow that orbit to grow and expand in its capabilities. At times it may only need one stroke in the water to steer to the left or right as the energy moves you. Apply the right amount of effort to change as you move out of the density of humanity. That density needs to be understood in what you experience as a person. For who does not feel offended at times? Who does not feel assaulted by words at various times? It is a quality in humanity, some of the ingredient used and reused in the play of human life.

So many humans are now being raised with so little money, so little resources. If you feel like one of them, you are not alone. And that is a major ingredient for the unrest and judgment in humanity that has been playing out for the eons. It's up to you to put that dance down. Are you willing to make the changes in your consciousness, the changes in your values to move out of that orbit? Would you dare move out of its orbit by giving more than you think you have? Stepping into a consciousness of abundance is having the guts to take a leap of faith knowing that the risk is everything. You are being vulnerable to the universe, and that is everything. You say, "Dear Universe, my beloved you are taking care of me. Whatever is in my pockets came from you. You will keep on giving and whatever is in my pockets moves on. I am free."

This is one path towards release and freedom. Can you lean into it? Can you lift yourself out of a well-used consciousness? Can you dismiss it and give up the identities around it? A big identity that they call the ninety-nine percent is now prevalent. Dismiss it. The one percent is here in consciousness. Evolve not by success, not by status but by living in freedom. Move out of the mediocrity, the crying and whining into the true, free nature that you are. Discover that the Lord of Your Being is the pot of gold. Social consciousness disguises the truth. It hypnotizes you and keeps you plugged in. Humans play this deception even in their games. You need to find a way to uplift from the state of the world as it is and from the way that your daily lives are put together. It is part of humanity's evolution to find a way to relate more authentically. It takes guts and sound determination to find your own voice.

There is a way to know if it is spirit that is animating your mind, if you are living in truth. You know by the level of spiritual thrill you are in. For the exhilaration of being in truth has no parallel. From there you can move out and be so completely taken by humanity's story. You are human and you know what it would be like to be in poverty, to live in a war zone. On some level you understand, so indeed your human self is tugged and pulled by compassion. The right application of effort is to let your heart go out to another, to send a blessing and just be human. Hold another in your mind and heart as if they are your dear sister and your dear brother. Hold them as someone who reminds you of your own child. Likewise, also hold yourself and your own child in your mind. Embrace those you hold dearly and be spiritual. Then, at the last breath you would say there is only eternity, and so it is.

The freedom and the winds of truth show you how magnificent an opportunity it is to be tested in a dream such as yours. So allow the many things to play out. Allow consciousness to dance in form, as you and around you. The manifest dance has hardness, thickness and it is sluggish. The unevolved come here and participate. And the ones who want evolution forgive them. In your world there are those actively forgiving war crimes upon their family. They are in the noble directive, seeing how ignorance plays out and being okay about it. They can recognize that ignorance plays alive and well in their own selves in little ways and sometimes in large ways. So, hold yourself and find a way to relate to others honestly.

Accept life as it is for in that you can taste forever. You taste forever as it lifts every cell of your body, as it lifts every hair on your head, as it animates your whole being. Truth has a way of validating itself and being recognized instantaneously. You can find the way to take your whole being and align it to truth. Allow it to teach you, deliberately calling on and deliberately falling into its wholeness. When you allow spirit to inhabit your life then it is easy and without effort. Matters fall together like you never thought they could. An energy is animating a universe that is in charge, orchestrating all things in a high vibration. When you fall into it, you discover that things are falling together. The body experiences that vibration and the chemicals in the brain are released as euphoria blossoms. You will know when you are in truth when the body/mind human is taken care of and escorted gently and appropriately into this experience. Then you will be set to take on whatever difficult teachings show up.

From infinite love we come and to infinite love we go with the message that you are infinite love as you are. Affirm this, know this, be this. So it is. Rhammah bids thee adieu.

INFINITY

For now, be the infinity that is holding you

Take a leap in knowing

Your anchor is conviction

Be cheek to cheek with all of life

Fall into life's stride and rhythm

Heal your relationship with yourself

For now, inhabit with the eyes of love, the ears of love,

and the heart of love

Discourse 5: I am Healing the Relationship with Myself

What do you have when infinite love finds its way onto the head of a pin? For now, the head of the pin is the Host and his mind-body. We use his intellect and ideas the best we can. Rhammah is forever-ness, a collectiveness of beings who know themselves as forever. And Rhammah is you in your original space, for you are eternity consciousness. To get a sense of eternity consciousness, you can look at the problems and concerns of this day. Think about your in-dividual story on this day and then think of a thousand years from now. Imagine yourself on a hilltop a thousand years from now. From there you might smell eternity a little better as the concerns of this day are a thousand miles away. Will you care? Will you give a hoot and be all wrapped up with those concerns? On that distant hill, will you be trying to outthink today as you feel backed into a corner with a dense process of worry?

As you sit here, we are asking you to anchor your mind and then project it a thousand years away. Now, turn yourself about and grab this form called you with both hands, just as eternity grabs this form with both hands. Think of two loving hands on your shoulders as you sit here. And be the form of infinity that is holding you. Hold your own body with the love of that thousand years of context. It is rather like being in your elder years and looking upon a little child with the compassion of age and wisdom. Hold your mind-body as eternity. Uplift it, be reverent to it and upgrade it with the context of your magnificence. Be the god that says, "Behold this lovely form gifted with function. It can speak, walk, talk and see. It can reach, pray and cry. Behold this awesome piece of beauty which is evidence of infinite love." Let that eternity rush in and imprint its love into the very fibers and cells of your body."

This is a chance of a millennia, this body and this moment. And we are asking you to consider that an exquisite and divine way can find its footing here. By saying yes to all that is here. Not only are we asking you to put both hands of your eternity on this body, we are asking you to put both hands of your eternity on this world and say yes to it. Behold creation in the four walls of this room, its floor and its ceiling. With the quiet resolve of that truth, imagine any circumstance you are in. If you can allow for this eternal being, you can hold both your body and reality lovingly. By doing this you quietly lift everyone. This occurs not because you grandstand in the front of the room. Neither does it mean you would crumble and cower to the back corner of a room. It occurs no matter where you sit because you say yes, this right here is evidence of the beloved Divine. This transformation happens by inhabiting the space with your whole being. You inhabit it with the eyes, ears and heart of love, with a lived way that says, "I am love."

What is your anchor? The anchor is the conviction, the absolute resolve. It is holding this body as an eternal being, insisting that problems are a thousand miles away. Reflect on this while each detail in your life is being done. Contemplate that the sense of problem is a thousand miles away in small simple moments, but also when your life goes amok and it seems to turn upside down. To an infinite being, things are always right side up. And the sense of problem is a thousand miles away. The anchor is conviction, and within you the capacity for knowing exists. Meditate, reflect, and get the answer. Go to sleep on it then wake up and get the answer. This knowing can be quantum. You can insist that every atom in the body is smiling and that the knowing is everywhere in your being.

You may wonder how to become more emotionally intelligent, healthier, more in harmony with others or more financially stable. Many beings walk their way through such challenges. They take risks. They retrain their minds and redo their budgets. So, how can you bend to circumstances? You know how to plan, but you can also throw out the plan or trade places for a new plan. Get better at each other's activity so that you will have more blending. Your abundance will be directly connected to your ability to coordinate in dynamic ways. One of you is good at organizing and another is more kid-like, light hearted. Trade places in such a way that you get each other. Each one of the beings here has very different patterns. You are all so unique compared to the other, so build a new life and walk into it. Or go into the original place and redo everything.

The discovery of the original place can be addressed through being on the hilltop. Sit on that stump here but know you are a thousand years away. Let the action of this day be whatever eternity is doing, what infinite love is doing. Action is revelation and whatever is said, whatever is done in this moment is an expression of divinity. Animating that action is done by giving with a blessing, giving with a gesture. We are asking you to take a leap into infinite vision, into the infinite love that is also immense power. It is the ability to be on, to be completely awake and completely free. You can do this while the spinning wheel of death goes on and on in the computer, on and on in the television. Be loving eternity while all hell is in the hand basket across the globe.

If you are stuck in traffic, stop the judgment created in that moment. Step into the eternity of a thousand years from now. Have great perspective and great distance from the current circumstances and be that eternal being with two hands on the shoulders of this body. Say, "Be still, this body is evidence of infinite love. Behold the beloved just as it is." When you are so free, do you know how brilliant your minds will be? The brain is so magnificent and so dynamic. The wholeness of your being when it uses your brain will be so brilliant because it is all energy. Project in your minds that, "All of the multitude of universes that inhabit each entity here, behold I call upon all that you are to align with the ultimate knowing that you are infinite love." Put yourself on this track and you will discover a magnificent, strident, deeply intuitive way of being.

Have you ever kicked down a door? Find a friend who has a dilapidated house that needs tearing down and ask him to give you the chance to kick down the door. Kick it down, stomp through it and say, "Hello I am here. I am infinite love." Say it to every room. Open every window and shout out each window. Say to the sun, "I am here with you in this house and I bless it with my presence. I am here as infinite love." Do this to uplift yourself. Say, "Silly mind, I love you but I am going to kick you down." Then enter the rooms of brilliance, of knowing, living and being. Say, "I am here to live, to embody infinite love. I shout it to the rocks, into the ground and say yes to all my faculties and use them."

This is the strident way. But there are those of you who need to start with minor adjustments. Wean yourself off your mediocrity. Do it slowly if you have to. Put the two hands on the shoulders and hold this body with the mind's eye. Say to it, "Evidence of the beloved, here you are and I am here with you. I will inch you off this bag of Doritos. We will go from two hours of TV a night to one. That's how much I love you. I know you do not like running, but we will walk around the block once. I know you are used to pizza, so we will eat spinach and then we will have pizza." Make deals, make deals with yourself, but do start. You are turning a part of you towards this stride as we encourage you to consider that it is yours. This living stride is in you. Say, "Hello new life. I will inch myself towards you. I might kick down the door or something in between. If I have to, I will crawl through the back window or go through the attic." Find your way, and breathe life into the dwelling of the being that you are.

There is also available to you an absolutely brilliant quantum breakthrough. For the spiritual brain is connected to the spiritual heart. And that is connected to your eternity which is connected to Allness in synchronicity. It is dynamic for you are a mind-body and you are a soul. But you are also eternity with the full knowing that is available. You have the ability to hold the pulse of divinity as it moves forth here on your planet. This is the edge of creation's crust with its frothing energy right here. Lean into that and say yes as an eternal being. Thank the cranky old door or whatever represents it in your life. Thank it as you kick it. Say, "I am practicing. I need the practice. I am a bit rusty so thank you for throwing this obstacle in front of me. I am going to kick this door down when I am ready, or else I will crawl in the back window."

If not that way, consider the quantum leap which is simply holding the whole dwelling in mind and allowing for the breeze to pass through every corridor. Allow for the fact that you are life on every level and life knows what to do. Life is animating every critter in your world. Every plant, every little piece of life is evidence of a brilliant knowing that is also in you. Wake up every morning and put your hand on your heart and own aliveness and newness each day. Say, "I am with you, I feel your pulse. I feel the pulse of all of life right here. Dear Lord, father, mother within come forth. Show me how to see with your eyes. Show me how to hear with your ears and speak your language that I may usher blessings to others through these lips. Breathe life into the moments of this day and help me see the hard turns for what they are."

You've called on Creator Source, now trust it. Trust it to blow its winds in such a way that the whole of you is lifted by the spirit within. Behold the adventure before you and walk into that mental place that feels the breeze on your cheek instead of the decay of yesterday. Walk quietly, prayerfully knowing that the sense of problem is a thousand years away. Humans can become affected when a friend, their beloved or a dear family member has moved on. But all of your friends and family from all of time are right here in your cells. Practice waking up and feeling the pulse of Oneness. Feel your dearest family members whether here or on the other side. Understand that both here and the other side is a story for a "me character," for a world invented for humans. Be an eternal infinite being, hold still and know. Allness is with you, it is here. There is a price you pay for stretching your consciousness into these human worlds.

You lose the conviction to hold your body with great love and to fully live here in service to your friends. If you can talk to your friends on the other side, they must be here. And if you can do so, so can she and he. Encourage others to listen inside themselves for that Oneness. Convince them that there is no problem, that it is all a thousand years away. Look at your own story as husband and wife, or in the dynamic of family and friends. Look at the circumstances and the tests. Then insist that you are on the hilltop a thousand years away. Insist on it and it can be as if one action handled everything. At this moment your one action is to send out a signal to the dream you have seen from your hilltop. You have a dream of harmony, of living a life that you do not know much about. Send a signal to walk courageously in that direction.

In this new adventure, the actual movement of power is coupled with fear. It also contains the fear of fear being gone. So ponder that for a moment. But living next to this is the eternity I am speaking about. Walk towards it and do not get lost in the many little pleasures and treasures. Get to that hilltop and find resolve. Be big and get real with yourself. Know what you want. Say, "I want to be cheek to cheek with all of life. I want to feel the thump of my spiritual heart when I live this day." It's okay to have a new car. It's okay to have a grand home and many friends. But it is much more likely that this would all happen for you if you got absolutely real about what you really want. What you really want is to live intensely and fully. And that vital living quality is attractive and absolutely dynamic. Creation's pulse and intention are within it, and as you fall into its stride and rhythm, you live on its crest.

We are doing better with this exercise of sitting on a stump and calling it a hilltop. It is like the anchor establishing what you are going to be. You will have great perspective and insist on integrity. You will align with clear action that is crackling with fear and power. We do not mean fear of life or any intimidation. We mean the lump in the throat quality of walking into this new adventure that is upon you. From a thousand years away you are saying behold the dynamics of this day and yes, give it to me. Do not sucker yourself into resistance and mucking yourself up. Change something. Wake up and get your butt moving. Change it up. It's about willingness, and not just any old willingness, but that's a start. Bring that determination even with the discomfort of a mind-body that is in pain. For some the mind-body has ailments, and there is an alteration in one's dream because they are less able. The mind can get turned in upon itself because of pain, discomfort and the fear of lost capacity. What does one do with that? It is a calling to hold one's self as eternity and to heal your relationship with yourself.

So, how does healing happen and what exactly is healing in such a circumstance? It is a state of being where you as eternity and you as a body-dream character are no longer two things. That is healing. The perception of those two ideas falls apart and there is only life. And the pain and discomfort keeps coming and the challenges to the dream keep coming. Strangely enough, that is a calling to wholeness that does not let up. How grand that situation is when you know you are eternity. As humans we must have compassion for these circumstances. But how beautiful and poetic that you would be called to wholeness so completely, with such an obvious message given so consistently. If you have pain, heal it now. Insist on knowing that the "lie of me" and wholeness of eternity are two things. Look at the awesome storms in your mind and emotional body and kick that door, that barrier down. You can heal it, so why not go for the gold? Be the one who is awake to this truth, moving through time and eternity and foreverness.

The Infinite Field of Love and the Great Ocean of Being are not two. In that understanding the stories disappear and the storms disappear. So while on one hand the anguish and the dance of conditioning continues, on the other hand there is a slow turning. Within you deals are being made because eternity is recognized. You are working it out, and while it may seem slow, each of you has a destiny with a miraculous renewal to wholeness. Lean forward into the promised land of heaven within. Lean into it and turn yourself towards it every chance you are able to. For each of you there is a time when it all falls together. It happens often when you do not need it to happen, and it is miraculous and profound. You earn it by moving in its direction in the way you are able to today.

Watch how many of your friends are looking for wholeness somehow, some way. And watch how few are able to find a place of wholeness as it is here now. Discover how to turn a piece of your being towards that. And when you can do that, another piece of you is no longer waiting for something to give you the answers, to fix you, cure you or give you a kick in the butt. From within you, the fire kicks you in the butt. And then the fire consumes more illusion. In your human experience fire burns out because it has a finite dynamic. The hottest flame uses the most fuel and disappears the quickest. But when you find your eternity, there is no end to its fire-like source. Its illumination fuels more within itself and magnifies. One little piece of the knowing we speak of today will be enough fuel to sustain a millennia of lifetimes. Just one fraction of the truth will sustain you joyfully.

And that is only a part of what is being offered here. Do you want to know what creates forever, what creates a universe and then another? It is divine intelligence in an immense, overwhelming system. And the probability for a planet to occur with the needed conditions for intelligent life to exist is staggeringly rare. So consider how powerful it is that you would appear here as a human. What are the odds that you would appear here in this room being reminded of your greatest nature, your eternity? How immensely miraculous for you to be given a pointer to what is available within you and to learn how to call on it. Are you going to sit at this seaside and only put your toe in the water? Wake up and hold your hand on your heart. Sit quietly enough to hear its beat and feel its energy as the emanation of life. That aliveness is your evidence of eternity.

Sit with that life as if it was the most exquisite babe. Say, "Dear Lord, Father, Mother of My Being, come forth and live this day. Bring forth a smile in every atom of this body. Allow me to quietly lift all beings in each moment. Give me the brilliance that is my birthright as I move out of the tick-tock of linear consciousness. Let me trust the brilliance of life as it uses my body-mind and upgrades its capacities. I step into this pulse of creation and live in its stride as a willing participant of Divinity. I am eternity. I am Infinite love. This body is its evidence. I honor it, take care of it and treat it with great love and reverence."

Just as Rhammah plays its way through the Host, so your divine identity plays its way through your body. Write down the prayers. You can rewrite them and make them work for you. Find your way to this truth we are speaking about. One little piece will hold you in joy for millennia, one tiny little piece. Get it, okay! Get it, indeed! We love you. We are so impressed with you. Rhammah bids thee adieu.

PART FOUR

VIBRATING WITH LIFE

EAGLE TRAINING

Let me see the vastness
Let me fill my lungs
Let me fill my wings
Let me walk forward off the cliff

What is under these wings?

What is it like to abide in the sky?

Sit empty.... Sit open

Be the bigness
Be the openness
Let your body be lifted

Soar into the sky
Soar among the clouds
Soar among the infinite

Instigate your own freedom!

You are like the wind taking the eagle

Discourse 1: Leaping into the Infinite Sky

We are taking away conditions of consciousness that weigh you down. Those programs given in life take you to places that inhibit your full expression. So, Rhammah brings you the whirling dervish. Let the assumptions you are fixed on whirl away into the dervish of your own whirling of energy. What answers are revealed as you are emptied and immersed in this warm, peaceful bath of energy? For your way unfolds in the aftermath, in the disappearance of all that binds you. What training must there be for you to spread your wings in a truly independent place? How much must you pick through in order to put your minds in this unfolded place? It is the vantage point where you can see the vistas like the soaring eagle. This is where the real you lives in the supreme love, infinitely peaceful, powerful and infinitely free reality.

Can you participate in the thrust that is the dervish and join its intention? Can you say many times in your day, "I give all to the loving grace that is everywhere, the loving energy that is power itself. I let it fill my lungs, fill my wings. I let it reveal to me visions. Beloved, I am open to Thee, so let the vastness be revealed." Then, something in you naturally walks forward off the cliff with your wings open. What is under those wings? And what is it like to abide in the sky? Ask yourself this in such a way that it shall be revealed. Ask, what is it like? And then sit open and empty, waiting for a revelation, a way. Breathe and allow your sinuses to be cleansed by the winds of your own nature, by your bigness and openness. Your body will be lifted when you know what it is like to be that power.

Experiencing this is a barometer. It is what you use to measure yourself up as you decide what to do, how to live, where to go and whom to be with. So activate that freedom. Give over all of your questions. Be empty and leap into the infinite sky. Your wings know how to cut through the wind and hold this form. Soar into the sky, amongst the clouds and infinite space. When things are seen from the great vastness, there is no confusion, no worry. Nothing is tangled. This stairway to the sky is reached by climbing one rock upon the other, one way, one school after the other. Get a fully rounded way and learn to dance full circle with humanity. Be able to befriend anyone and have affinity while disagreeing. What must you discern to address all the worries of the mind? You twist and turn thinking about how to be, will this career work, should I be here, am I doing enough? Is there a school for me to move forward, to grow in? Is there a healer that might do it for me, a modality or a trick that will fix things?

These are all things that you have to work with. Find a real place to establish your footing. For there is a time when you need to make an assessment and say, "Am I going to lift my foot onto a boulder that I'm not used to? Can I go to a place that asks me to question everything in my consciousness?" Climb to that place where you can stand on both feet. From there you will look back and not quite recognize yourself. On that new plateau, from that new vista on the mountain you can see full circle. The many schools of wisdom point to various heights of the self. They encouraging you to prepare for the great launch into the sky. You must position yourself to look upon the abyss, for everything that got you there eventually you must leave behind. But at this juncture, fly and reference the authority that is aliveness, the natural essence of what you are. Reflect on its power and let it take you.

Okay, so you hear this and commit to moving forward. But you wonder about feelings, emotions and the play of choices in being human. After climbing many rocks towards the great heights and going through many layers of the same old truths, one contemplates the very real and overwhelming activity of humans. You will not become separate from this. If anything, the emotions and connections with others become more infinite. Consider whoever is on your bus, in the next room, your family by blood or association and those dearest to you. In this elevated embodiment of your foreverness, you will be with them cheek to cheek. When you feel the universe, you will feel their universe. You will feel their multitudes, their sense of "what about me" in every dimension. And yet, again and again something in your belly says, "And there is also forever."

There is this kinship, this family that you have captured here. It is a family of souls flocking. So, be with your neighbors knowing they have their struggles. For your nature instinctually reaches out and feels. It can be haunted by all of humanity, by the wars and the great trials, by the duties inflicted upon the unwilling. Because of circumstances, some are forced to be bureaucrats in a system that is inhumane. These are examples of the trials of humanity. Indeed, you can be with all of this human emotion, but on each step up know that the emotion does not go along. It disappears as you evolve. It is so, and your way of being with all of it becomes easier as your reference point draws nearer to the infinite freedom that you are. You realize that in your being there is the dance of falling into thickness and moving through it. Revelation opens you and unfounded worries disappear in this new day. A new day and a new way is taking you like the wind takes the eagle to new heights.

This new way, the kinship and friendship with the universe is a leap of faith. It is a calling. For some, everything is dropped as they rest in a cave of consciousness. For others they write books and go on the lecture circuit. So what does it mean for you? For each, at different times it means different things. There are steps and many paths alongside the mountain you will climb. Some pathways drift

158

and meander before they make their way back up to the highest peaks. As humans, you have all gone the longer way for periods of time via diverted thinking. But you have carried along your wisdom, so the compass is still set. Eventually you look for that next step towards greater reality. You will know it because it is alive in you. It is contemplated against the great question within you. Even if that next step is spontaneous, all you need is an instantaneous reference to the power of your being. Giving yourself over to wisdom allows it to take you into the sky. That day comes at different times for different beings, but it eventually comes for all.

You are all souls from many lives. And you are eternity, foreverness, the embodiment of infinity itself. Being all of these at once can create a type of confusion when the embodied one of now is embraced. But this struggle, when infused by the wisdom can become harmony. The spiritual brain activates and handles those movements beyond the tracks of the human brain. There is a shift to where you can handle the dichotomy of your foreverness. It's like you hold these two parts, one in each hand. You hold them until there is no problem with that in your consciousness. When this happens it means you've moved out of cycling in humanness. You have found a new orbit with your spiritual brains and the etheric knowing about your bodies. There is a capacity to orbit in new ways with all that unfolds. And when the simple teaching of supreme kindness becomes profound and deep it will blow your mind. From that place, there is so much love for the game of humanity participating full force in its dance. You can go into that dream all the way, with both hands and keep your eternity.

In these lessons we teach you about an eternity that it is also about evolving as you move forward life after life, after life. From the birth of your soul in almost forever ago there was something like spiritual DNA. That initial gesture that is your soul still remains as spontaneous as it was in the beginning. This initial spontaneous bluster is there even after eons. Its qualities continue on as it becomes various frames of being. For indeed, you are a quality of the Divine like blue is a quality of the light spectrum. As a spontaneous aspect, a radiance of the One you behold each individual lifetime. There is a signature about the whole of your life. There is a nuance when you've thrown your mind upon the many years of your existence. A quick glance into that flash, that vision is like sitting with the initial flash of your soul's creation eons ago. Looking upon this reflection, you can let the gestalt of your world remain. It becomes like viewing paint spontaneously thrown on a canvas as your consciousness sits with your eternity on the edge of creation.

Embrace this step. Look upon yourself with an easy going gaze, a relaxed impression of self. A non-literal way becomes the seat of your being, but in this you don't abandon your human involvement. This lesson is a training exercise, so please balance your taxes accurately, write your name one letter at a time when necessary and list your social security number when required. Recall specific details of your past when necessary. Emotionally and energetically, there is wisdom in dancing with specific details of your lifetime. But in the belly of your being, hold this wisdom and don't get completely lost in the details of a lifetime. And also understand the massive power that is available from this connection. There is a device in the human protecting you from knowing this power, and without this device it might be rather precarious to reference your eternity. The nature of that will be revealed when it is time.

Being with yourself in this sense is like the hands are off the steering wheel. With your foot on the gas something in your being moves. It can propel you, and it is wise to have built a foundation of integrity and right action before you engage it. In the beginning, there was the infinite dimensionless, and there were many souls flickering like candles. They were impressions like a signature of DNA sent out to play forever, FOREVER! This power behind them is like a fire that can burst and encompass miles of a forest, then reduce itself to an ember. In your vastness, you are the ember, and you are the many lights. You are the fire in the forest and the individual in that chair. You are that and you are multitudes, one flicker of energy traveling through many lives being simultaneously every drop of this planet. This is a truth which takes those who are ready into a new orbit with themselves and all that is. Don't fear to embrace this power, for you can handle it. It might make your head hurt a bit, but you can handle it.

Can you see how you are moved by this teaching? Turn towards it and you give to yourself and others this exquisite gift. Something in the energy of this room needs to be shouted into yourselves until you spread those wings and are alive with this truth. Do not wait. Thank yourself now for being here, for offering this time to listen. It is profound how Rhammah values your gifts. Rhammah is drunk with love for your grand, magnificent gifts. And why not let it appear profoundly simple, humble and real while within yourself you value it like the shiniest jewel one has ever polished. Honor the fact that you would show up here and be with the wisdom that takes the "ME" out of your identity of self. We ask you to be so open that the step forward asks for everything to be given and to be new. And in that, everything is revealed. We look upon you with Rhammah's gaze and engage the many pockets of energy around and behind your being. They need to be spoken to this way.

Indeed, all of the work Rhammah is doing, you can also do. You too can be of service just sitting in public and using this wisdom to change the energetic environment. Talk to your neighbor in silence. Be amongst the multitudes and value their nature, their innate existence through silent affirmation of this truth. Honor that nature which burst forth in the birth of their soul, that DNA like stuff with its flickering of divine energy. Look into the multitudes with the whole of your being, beholding all that they are. Behold the many human spaces of anxiety, of yearning for greatness, for truth, and always wanting things to be more. Abide in such a way that you relax into them and also relax into all that you are.

Within this affection, the power is available to stretch the energy and move it into a new orbit. When the conscious mind moves into a new orbit inside of itself, it also does that inside of infinity. Indeed, these words may confuse you unless you are earnestly moved to be with them in a new way. However, something in you knows how to work with all of this. So, close your eyes, relax into the body of energy and continue this work. Hold this power, for it will always be there unconditionally, immediately available for you. Bless all beings that come to mind with this infinite nature that is spontaneous. Give yourself to it, "One Source, one way, spontaneously alive.............. (*pause*) It is time to ask yourself how to be with the nature of this planet, with how people are and what they do, with how they think, with their politics and with their various beliefs and choices.

Can you be sending a greater blessing to all without exception? Know when there is a movement, when an offering needs to be made. Also know when to be quiet and allow another's truth to reside. That is the profound big mystery in you, and how divinity works. To sit for eternity with someone who doesn't agree with you, that is how big your nature in Source is. You know when the person next to you needs a little word, a lot of words, or tough words to instigate results and growth. Sitting on a rock is not the only destiny of the Universe. All of these suggestions may confuse many humans, but it won't confuse one who abides in the Wisdom of True Source. This is your reminder from head to toe, to be versatile. Work with this, school is in session. Rhammah bids thee adieu. Thank you, great masters.

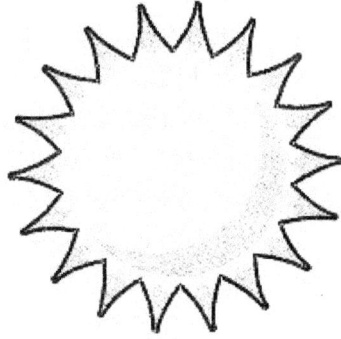

QUANTUM BRILLIANCE

How magnificent the human way is

How massive its weaving of layers

For the human is an evolutionary miracle

How are you part of it all?

Dynamic, forming, evolving

Infinitely solid…..Infinitely elastic

Discourse 2: Where You Want to Be

In the same way a leaf discovers the wind you are here to discover truth. Rhammah brings a fellowship of masters who are pure, undivided infinite love and they affirm what is to come in your commitments and vision. There is guidance available, and you all have the capacity to be a part of "how knowing works." For you can be in resonance with your oneness and hear the whispers of truth. Many humans are stuck on their necessity to hear answers like does he love me, or does he love me not? Will I get the job or will I make the grade? But much in life is a crapshoot, so consider allowing life itself show you how to be with life. Learn how to be light hearted in peace and grace. What if the wind blew in such a way that it said, "Stop looking for answers. Be with me. Here we go." The wind is a fine metaphor for life as it is constantly saying, "Here we go." It is taking you unavoidably to the new adventure. And there is this capacity to respond to that because life speaks to you in ways that the human context cannot decipher or decode.

As humans you are incarnated to be with those in your life who might hire you, parent you, couple with you or just ask you questions. If you carry this greater truth, when they come to you from where they are at you might be able to take them to new places. It may not be done philosophically. You might simply acknowledge what a grand being they are. You can appreciate what they have done to get where they are at. With some you might discuss beliefs or philosophical views. But you also come from an understanding that the most well researched, perfectly constructed philosophy of living is only useful for a temporary period of time. And it can be a real quandary for humanity that they will not survive if they don't make necessary adjustments in their vision and understanding. Reshaping, researching, drawing new conclusions is an important part of human and social function.

You will find this to be true in researching foods, remedies, medicines, how to raise children, what are the fashion trends or the best educational methods. It is also true of beliefs and their reformulation. The human mind is constantly weaving and the human being is an evolutionary miracle. In your millions of years of evolution, childhood has arrived to a place where it takes about twenty years for you to learn how to survive and hopefully function in your social jungle. And good as it may be, it can also be quite messy. Your so called reality has the qualities of elasticity. It is similar to the movie screen with the infinite variety of images, textures, colors and ways of unfolding that appear. Your living movie is even more complex and rich, for there is smell, taste, touch and sound. There are also intuitive qualities and senses beyond the main five human senses.

The movie screen that is life and the play that you are, these are really something to reckon with. In addition, you have the human capacity for very complex ways to put it together complete with strategies, philosophies and research. Your historical, spiritual, scientific, clinical and theoretical conceptions are all quite magnificent. For the human way is absolutely awesome, a massive weaving of layers that you are a part of. Human conditioning sets you up for function and movement. It is magnificent but can also be a virtual stewpot that seems to work, but can many times end up being crippling. Your human capacity for reflection and perception fosters a tenacious habit of holding on to patterns, assumptions, conclusions and judgments. These contribute to much that traps and confuses you. Many get stuck, repeating human lifetimes over and over in this conundrum.

But you have the possible option to live a dynamic life where your whole being is elastic, where it can move and evolve in an infinite number of ways. This movement is dynamic, forming and collapsing. There is a constant breakdown and re-forming. To one who is not activated spiritually this is more difficult, for the change produced by this process is deeply threating to a persistently conditioned setup. It challenges a way of being that is fixed, which can lead to conflicts and strife in human systems. So it is important to understand that humanity was not designed for fixity. It was designed to put together, experiment with, try, discover and also put things down. In your journey, whole new notions can be experimented with and put down. There is nothing wrong with this. The Divine is not ever angered by this, for it is the very design of creative intelligence, the innate ability of Creator Force.

All existence has the capacity for what we might call quantum brilliance. In manifest plays, an adventure is afoot where one's being is given to infinite power and excellent grace. Rhammah is verbally paying homage to the vast complexity of all existence and also to your existence, the many layers of what you are. You are alive energetically, intellectually, psychically, emotionally and in the dance of karma. And there are many more layers than these few we mention, layers you cannot fathom. The Creative Divine is that power, that intelligence which is emoting all of it. And by contacting and abiding in the aliveness that is animating everything, this whole teaching can be known instantly and intuitively within your being. A thousand books could not come close to what can be discovered by simply absorbing the sublime truth we share here now.

So focus on the alive, exquisite energy. It is here. It is in the wind to be discovered, so make contact with it. Doing this with attention and affection will be liberating. For the wind can send a boat sailing across the sea. And the grace that is life can send forth the many aspects and layers of your being. The complexity of this is miraculous and ingenious. At its heart there is exquisite, powerful simplicity. It is gentle, enchanting, eternal, solid like granite but free like a bird's feather on the wind. This energy has both elasticity and solidity and in order to be related to there must be duality. You reflect on a feather and you reflect on a rock. That's what the human being understands. This energy has a poetic quality when you discover its way and its truth. Infinitely solid and infinitely elastic, how could that even be? Such a statement confounds the human mind. How could granite be infinitely elastic? How could a feather be like granite?

This puzzle cannot be solved with your mind. You have to sit with your heart and your intuitive core. As discovery comes little by little it can shift you, making life a bit easier. As you awaken to these truths, there will be a resounding celebration that you are simply alive. And realizing the fact that life is a spiritual miracle can change you. It can break down the greedy areas of your consciousness, the selfish traits in your being as you discover new models of operation. Your ego can discover that it is easier to get what it wants through having a good attitude, an ingenious mind and adventurous spirit. There are ways to get what you want through behavioral evolution. So, let the infinite energy of divine love show you the way to new ideas in human culture. Let it show you how to establish ideas that are powerful and free. Be divinely guided regarding which ideas to pick up at the right time and place. Also be guided and shown how to put them down when they become destructive or harmful.

Humans have a tendency to move through life in a sequential way. You tend to singularly track how a body moves or a storyline unfolds. So it can be challenging to embrace and pay attention to the evolution of the many dimensions that you are. But as you slip through to multidimensional expressions, there is the ecstatic thrill of allowing a freeform play of ideas to be experienced. You can live life ecstatically and discover this eternal dynamic. And what does that look like? It might go like this. Say that you are playing vegetarian, exploring all the different things created in that definition.

167

But within the parameters of that philosophy, you would not dare make it into a religion or mandate. You would experiment with being vegetarian as if you know that in two years you are going to explore the world of meat. There would be an understanding of the impermanence and you would not be stuck in attachment. So feel free to allow new types of parameters. Discover new set-ups and be flexible enough to put one down and try another and another.

Many choices for your focus can find harmony in your vast globe of human expression. For example, it is not wrong to commit to one thing, like a chef to a lifelong endeavor to be a genius cook in the French cuisine. It can be right. And there is evolution in that if it is taken lightly, if it is an art done in freedom. But doing one path and then changing to another can also be right. So understand that living life with this elastic posture sets you up to be able to handle change while times are volatile. In your current times many humans do not know which way they are going or what is to happen next. Many are blind to how they might be evolving in reference to how they choose to operate in the human arena. As we said, change can be deeply threatening to a persistently conditioned mindset. So ponder deeply that such fixity is not really the basis of creative design. It is not how God operates, not what is required. Understanding this revelation, human spirits and minds must work together to embrace diversity and evolution.

Be excited by the workings of the mind while your gravity is in your spiritual center. Your mind is intended to be a servant to that center. Occurrences of the moment are opportunities to reflect on the true light and its movement. For example, it can be exciting to diagnose a terrorist through the various intellectual frameworks. (*Prior to the session the group was discussing a recent mass murder incident in the U.S.*) It can be useful to find a way that brings you meaning, gives you guidance and relieves your suffering. It is useful indeed. When your brothers and sisters are being harmed it is not easy to bear. You feel called to find meaning in life when it is dark and painful. You want to choose a way of seeing it that makes you feel better. In your limited human perception that can be useful. But there is also a dimension of yourself that can see everything as energy. Even a seeming destructive occurrence can be viewed as the alive, God-like energy playing. That dimension of yourself sees everything as God and as Light. It is as if it is undulating, moving in ways similar to how areas of your planet are shifting. Plates under the surface are moving and shifting. How that looks on the surface of Earth is different than the dynamics underneath the surface where larger designs are at play.

The human mind, schooled in notions of right and wrong struggles with this type of concept. But if humanity is shifting in many ways and there are things going on underneath, you will not be able to remedy that or figure it out. And why should you if you know it is just life moving with itself, being with itself in new ways. You can be a part of this new way that "life is with itself" by embracing the truth in your day. Embrace a new spiritual way of being with it. Be a blessing even under the most trying circumstances. Pass your tests. Stop groveling, griping, whining, groaning and moaning. Stop trying to figure it all out. Track the tone of energy that is in your being. Ask yourself if the way you are living allows the winds of truth to hit your sails. Let every question you are asked or questions that you hold in mind be what calls you forth into speech and into action.

It can help you in this mindset to know that humans are where they want to be. Whatever their story might seem to validate, they are not actually limited by it. Rather they are simply where they want to be. It is always easier watching someone from a distance. They may be groveling in their mind, sad in a way that is conditioned, but they are where they want to be. And again the human mind struggles with this. It is the rare soul who says, "Forget what this human wants, it is time to live in joy." For human conditioning is threatened by someone living in joy who is busting at the seams. That kind of joy goes headfirst into life. It's always trying new things. It will not let yesterday's events take away today's exuberance. The energy of the Divine lives in joy and it lives in the moment. No matter what, it sees the entire picture and embraces it in ecstasy.

So sit right here and now in this energy before your mind can get in the way. The intensity of presence is made easier by the fellowship here and the help of the masters. They are with you, standing behind you, supporting and holding you. You can take that support with you as you go. So sit with these sublime concepts and watch how the mind is trying to come in and take over. Like a blanket of darkness, it tries to creep in and smother the wisdom. So resist and hold this wisdom's intensity and alignment. Hold your affection for its energy. It is being generated in such a way that the shroud of conditioning is having a harder time crawling on you and taking over.

When there is not enough alignment, the teaching folds away. It becomes an underused, underfed quality. As conditioning crawls over a person it can become despair, hopelessness, dismalness, aggravation, confusion, etcetera. It corrupts you by suggesting that you need to figure everything out or need to be a certain way to feel safe. We are suggesting that now is the time to warm yourselves in the presence of truth. Let it seep in so that it is called forth and becomes an innate way. Put your hands up like you are around the fire. (*Rhammah demonstrates.*) Feel the energy in your body and the warmth radiating from the group. Warmth is creeping in to your skin, your bones and to the many dimensions through the energy of affection, through dedicating yourself to this mindset's energy. Now bathe your bodies with this energetic light." (*Rhammah demonstrates the action of moving the hands as if one is smoothing and spreading the light over all of the body.*) Wash to the feet, work it in, scrub, scrub everywhere. Scrub the rubbish loose and allow it to slide off and go to the Earth. This is a thing of power, keeping your gaze up, indeed. School is in session. Rhammah bids thee adieu.

ONENESS

Infinite, primordial essence

Reflected upon itself

Played in the garden of subtle reality

Testing itself out, within itself

Oneness began dancing

Moving forward as evolution

Consciousness emerged

Infinite intelligence

Infinite oneness

Discourse 3: Wisdom of Choice and Universal Structure

(Prior to the session a participant asked whether everything is pre-ordained by a higher power or if we as humans have a free will and are able to make choices that can alter the course of events and our lives. From this question, a rather lively pre-channeling discussion ensued with various layers on this theme.)

There is the story of the infinite, primordial essence which is Oneness. It reflected upon itself and became many. Then it played in the garden of subtle reality, of subtle consciousness, testing itself out within itself. Oneness began dancing in infinitely subtle ways in its infinite intelligence. There was greater and greater complexity at work moving forward as evolution from very subtle pulses to greater and greater density. Finally, consciousness emerged as form in one celled creatures, and so the story goes. There was infinite intelligence behind even the one celled creature. The manifest divine intelligences worked in committee with what was the very crest of creation's tide. Infinite Oneness moved forth into complexity. It entered into greater density, contemplating within itself to go further and further into a deeper dream.

From that continuance, here you are. The One has given you a dream on a planet with great diversity, with awesome complexity and layers of consciousness. In that story, there are some humans who are denser than others. Their density can consist of "me against you" to the utmost degree. Hate and cruelty are perceived by them as necessary, useful tools. Such beings are allowed. They need to be in their positions. And this is one way of explaining how The Absolute is playing with and within itself. It plays in the many colorations and the many textures and qualities of itself. It is infinite and multidimensional in a sense, while it also isn't. As real as it is, it is also not real. For it appears in a quantum fashion, flickering on the perception of an observer.

Philosophical inquiry into these statements can hurt your brain. But such pain burns away the onion skin layers of your own humanity. It goes about delivering you to the One. This pain can be the egoic need for understanding or the very literal pain of the body. In a study like this of ultimate wisdom, you must be prepared to reference everything as one and the same, everything! But of course, in the life of a human there are layers that need to be handled on the level that one is at. And so, the perceived realm of choice is used as a deliberate part of that game. It must be played through, dealt with in the human dreamscape that seems visceral and real.

The realities of an easy human life and a difficult human life need to be seen for what they are at face value. Human perception must choose what remedy is to be used. When you seek a source of wisdom for both healing and perspective, you come for answers that are both for the human and for the infinite self. And when Rhammah says to you, "Live stridently as truth," he speaks to the greater nature that does so without command. That greater nature can go to great truth when there is nothing in the way. Does that occur even when you are not awake? In some sense yes, but mostly in those of unacknowledged awareness it does not. So, we must hint that the power and spontaneity to live in truth is in you. For, the moment when a soul awakens cannot be preordained. It is a spontaneous event. That's why we work with you at the various levels where you are. And you must find out how to balance both arenas.

So, hold your own hand and look at your journey as a character in a dream. Ask yourself, "Have I been treated compassionately? What answers were useful for the time when I suffered?" Know that the answers and the choices you've made in the past are of a dream character that you are not as intimately entwined with now. From that perspective, it is easier to see how your choices were all necessary. You may understand how the aching helped you reach for wisdom. It is part of the play and included in the game of smoke and mirrors. The smoke and mirrors are organized in order for this dream to seem real to you. Just as in this dream, the personal experiences of pain and difficulty often create contractions. They create a "why me" attitude and torturous angst.

So, how do you see your way through that? For life presents itself and it is not all easy. You must work with it just as it is, just as you are now. But understand that your higher philosophical nature coexists with the physical circumstances. And in time that higher philosophical nature will become a part of daily choice. Ultimately, you might understand that it was always there and these dual perceptions are not separate. The sense of them being separate was only occurring in your perception. It is like that for us too as we attempt to explain this concept. We cannot speak to you about the full reality because of the limits of your perception. We must speak of one and then the other aspect that can be integrated by the light of your inner consciousness as it discovers the meaning of this wisdom.

This is a reality that is better discovered than taught. Allow the masters to whisper into your ear and don't intellectually try to figure all of this out. The beauty of truth is in the release of a contracted human who is trying so hard. Many of the questions you have raised are pointing to the potential of transcending one's current reality. You want to know how to allow it to be, how to make choices guided by the intuitive self. Can you be okay with one answer being necessary for a period of time and then another answer comes along? Can you allow it all to be the ordained way the knot undoes itself?

In the story of The One playing in itself and dancing in the many realities of density, you are a presentation. Your life and all you see and experience is a presentation of evolution. And you are participating by your own volition, by what seems to be your own choice. If you find yourself in what you define as a difficulty, what comes with that is a sense of me. That sense of me has an automatic sense of choice and we are asking you to use it wisely. You ask, "How do I deal with this pain? How do I deal with this emotion, this sense of difficulty? How do I deal with it?" Because the question is there, the sense of effort must be used. If you are awakened, then nothing is necessary.

In the awakened state, the sense of me is gone and nothing is needed. It all just unfolds. There is a possible point in your journey where you can see that the concept of negativity is totally gone, but positivity is also totally gone. You will just see the best a human can do in any given moment. In that vision, freedom is provided, nothing is personal and reality is beyond negative and positive. It is a freedom where everything is fine and all is well. If that's not real for you yet, then you might have to consider how your fellow members in traffic have agendas. You may need to take the remedy necessary according to the level of the hook. But know, what seems to be personal is really the ultimate aspect of the dream. When you are watching a movie, you have only sight and sound. But in human dimensions, you are experiencing all the senses and a range of emotions. The personality is hooked into seeing everything as personal with the identity contracted and concerned for itself.

To totally undo that, you must be without caring for how it plays out in your individual life while on the other hand, your lives do matter. They completely matter. Your good fortune matters and you need to care about it, otherwise you would fall apart. There is an appropriate time to use a teaching. But, you need to tend to yourself and raise yourself as you would your child. However, your ultimate destiny is in a deeply impersonal life where everything is seen as no problem. Respect how few people ennoble themselves and strive to get there. In some ways, it is dangerous to do so. In other ways, it is so compelling that one must go on the quest of this expanded wisdom.

For you, this presentation sits between several visions of wisdom and appears as a paradox. You may prefer a non-paradoxical, clear-cut teaching that appears black and white. But such teachings do not incorporate all wisdom and generally have less adaptable concepts. They have some value and can suit many people. But you are the alive, intuitive being who can balance and interpret expanded wisdom. Within you is the force that can work with the mental paradoxes of such teachings and evaluate their value for yourselves. If that force is not awake in you, you will be confused. Ask for that ability to be awake and point your efforts towards it.

You can affirm, "Oh Lord of My Being, the source before all sources, I ask you to come forth. Show me how to be with my life in good stewardship, even while I know it's not as real as I think it is. Show me how to be kind and grateful with my psychology, my material life and this physical body in such a way that I am aligned to transcendence. Show me how I can allow for the highest way of seeing this life. Teach me how to coexist with the complexity and redirect my attitude. Show me how that presence which calls forth conscious effort is in charge. Bless me that I may choose conscious efforts, choose higher wisdom and all that is necessary for the turnaround of my spiritual evolution."

Living fully open requires doing it all within the elaborate smoke and mirrors play inside of your own mind. The Source of all sources can balance that out. You have it in you to claim what is necessary for each day. Discover the spontaneous miracle where all choices are seen through. Yet, within this framework what appears to be choice and earnestness exist. So, why not be disciplined? Why not have character? It is a potential in Source to have a pattern running. It is also a potential for unhelpful patterns to be in play. And these two potentials can shift. You may ask about who is in charge as you are given circumstances. You have the imperative to put forth effort to turn around resistance, to turn around a bad attitude. The god of life is choosing that turn around. So know that you are that god.

The most awakened state is to know that things are never a problem. But within that medications are given, healings are given, and people are cared for in their pain. With your best efforts, listen in compassion, give remedies and give care. Is there not a place for all of it? Additionally, care about yourself and give yourself what is necessary. Understanding this requires even more of a posture to see truth from the highest perspective. You can see it all as Source, the cigarette, the smoker, the doctor, the pills are all simply Source. View the layers of your own consciousness as Source playing out. See how it flickers in the many colors and textures, qualities and impressions. If you can, focus your effort to consciously bring forth that intuitive knowing. You are well on your way.

Affirm, "Dear Lord, Source of My Being, show me how to be with this day. Show me how to be real with what is presented." If you are presented with a contraction around your "Me" identity, let the Lord of Your Being say, "Look at your sense of choice in the personal. And look at the intention to transcend it. Apply effort to see through it." If you have a pain in your psychology, your body, in relationships, or in your life you may have to find a more appropriate medicine. But know that these bigger truths are in your back pocket. They are the inevitable destiny that you are moving towards. And if this higher way is in your back pocket, everything that happens is what is necessary for that discovery to unfold.

It is good to listen to this teaching, but directly discovering that the needs of the ego are not necessary is better. You are allowed to ruminate on this and taste the freedom in this realization. Your questions will eventually move to a different level and any sense of suffering will shift to a different level. In the discovery of the One, you see that there are many levels. The mind wonders how this can all be so. Try not to over think it. Find a way for this alive, moving set of teachings to massage you brain so you are prepared for truth on a gut level, and also on energetic levels. Be still. Be still and allow. Be prayerful on how to apply effort. For applying effort to not being in effort is a nosebleed situation. It is problematic all by itself, is it not?

Wisely affirm that you are infinite love. It is of great use to say, "All that can be quantified by human perception is limitation. I dismiss it. It will not rule this day. In the light of the truth of infinite love I dismiss all concepts." Deeply allow that inside of infinity, all things are included. The dream character, its karma, its family and the sense that there are beings coming and going in this world lie within the Infinite. The entire energetic matrix that is this world and all that lies just outside of it is also included. To find a way of being with this is Buddha like. It is a great quest and a fantastic experience to have all this unfolding within you. The struggles and breakthroughs of personality, even the contractions and transcendence are not a problem.

Know that the mechanics of your manifest dream have to be supported by intelligence and many divine beings. But as an infinite being, there is only one God, one Source in charge. Be okay with this. It plays out in you and there is an appropriate dharma unique to you. This is a most beautiful discovery, a magnificent way to frame big truth and all the many truths that are allowed to play out within it. Say to yourself, "I am infinite love and all that plays out within that is fine. Now I relax as infinite love. I am infinite love and the matters of this dream character are handled as if they matter or as if they don't matter." There is a wisdom and a skillfulness that makes this work. Things are played out while they are seen in the greater perspective and they are no longer so important.

Other humans might think a person in this state is vague because this or that are all just fine. However, in infinite consciousness, everything is just dancing. Will you allow yourself to dance this dance? And for the pain that screams, you answer like you would a child's scream. You would take care of what is at work because you are infinite love. Love is what you are and it is what you do. As infinite love, the karma of this body/mind still plays out. It still has issues, but they are playing out in the great ocean of love. The twists and turns have a reference which somehow loosens the contraction. Knowing the greater nature is a wonderful medicine, for many things cannot occur in a state of duality and resistance.

Imagine yourself like a martial artist. Each hand cuts differently and has different capacities. On the one hand you say, "Cut the crap. You have been at this long enough. Be alive and stop being such a human. Don't be lazy about awakening. Get beyond the ego." That hand is swung. It is used in full force on yourself for you are the one being who can use it most completely. Then, on the other hand you say, "Treat yourself with love. Get some rest. Don't worry so much. Acquire some friends. Get some TLC. Take a hot bath or take a vacation, it's okay." That hand is swung in the other direction and they both work together as they stir consciousness. The compassionate self is tender and caring as it works alongside the great sword of truth. Get used to both hands.

You are like beautiful birds in a bamboo cage living in a lovely forest and seeing the truth all about you. It is a tight cage of human conditioning and you must learn to love the cage. Be appropriate with it and heal where necessary. This greater truth is the beauty of your feathers, the beauty of your song and the beauty that is truth in the forest of your being. In the struggle with your sense of being caged by human limitations, be with that dilemma as if it is okay to stay forever. Heal it and be okay with the tools of this world, for your true nature is of another world. Ask yourself to find the balance between these worlds. Find harmony in your transcendence, for there is harmony and it will be delivered to you by Source. In due time, the acorn falls from the tree. You will choose it in the alignment that is spoken about in this teaching. We are very impressed with all of you. You are doing very well. Rhammah bids thee adieu.

NEEDLE AND THREAD

Hold in mind a needle and thread

Hold that vision
In your mind's eye

Find that needle
Find that thread

Stitch your way through all the things that come up in you

Discourse 4: Embracing the Thread of Unity

There are those who live in one world where one kind of wisdom works, and others live in a world where a different wisdom works. Rhammah represents the common thread of all who are here. So hold in mind needles and thread as the vision of this evening. With this vision of creation in mind, imagine yourself sitting at the crest of this moment's wave and peering into what is about to come. For your cells to dance and your electrons to harmonize with this vision there needs to be a single pattern in place. Project this vision of reality as a pattern in your world moving forward, evolving, shifting and changing. There are those who constantly contribute to that vision by giving their best, their highest nature and by calling on all faculties.

So in your mind say, "I give myself over to this group and the energy of this evening so that there will be unity and an unfolding that gives victory for all." For there are those of you here who need to go on a hero's journey to overcome obstacles. And there are others who need to see through the apparent reality of being human. Do these intentions coexist? Can they be one on some level? Indeed, when you are seeing past your false, limited perceptions, past your "I can't attitude," victory is possible. A false, limited perception such as "I can't," is just as false as thinking there is a "me." It's as fundamentally untrue as thinking "I am real as an ego" or "I am real as a dream character." There are victories to achieve on entirely different levels and they are a dismissal of limited perception, of that which is not real.

What you see as humans is like light flickering on the water. You can watch how humans get lost in the images, in the gestalt of human perception. They get lost in life's myriad dysfunctions which unfold from seeing one's crap in the mirror of the waters. A great tangle of blaming comes from this because your brother, your sister, even the fellow humans who appear in your day can represent wounds from early life. On some level it is all a conversation with your own memory. You are vulnerable to yourself and to believing your human mind. So one common thread is, don't believe your mind. For this quest it is entirely useless. When this becomes an actual reality for you, you will see through the dance of the mind. Then you move into a state of revelation.

In the revelation of truth, your energies and all the various parts of you live in an embodiment of perpetual bursting. Your thoughts and all of your identity goes into servitude towards this bursting revelation. Instead of seeing yourself as an object, as a human with a story, now there is the revelation of expansive energy. You are part of living spiritual fire. And all that moves and functions is simply the aliveness dancing as this fire, living in the veins of all reality in every object. To see reality in a chair is different than asking, "Why is there a chair? Why is there a sun? Why is there a moon?" In revelation, the heart thumps at the very moment a sea of stars emerges in the sky or the waves hit the rocks. One's whole being can vibrate in the glee of aliveness. There is no why in that state. There is only the knowing of life at work through your own veins, through every gesture. Life comes forth from your being and courageous, heroic components emerge in that revelation, in that embodiment of life.

Judgments can interrupt this image of life's layers being simply reflections on a pond. You are vulnerable for getting caught up in this reflection, for you are in this active game with friends, family, your circumstances, etcetera. You are unaware that your own memories are playing out in your day. They are in your sense of abandonment and estrangement, in every situation where you are a blatant, obvious victim who was wronged. But, in all of this, it is possible to step back and watch the larger play at work. See the teachings that are life viewed from the depths of wisdom. And that depth is best actualized through disappearing into the fire and luster of your spirit. When you move from fear into energy alignment and the release of entropy, your fear may go into anger. You must be able to see through that hall of mirrors which includes resentment, holding grudges, seeing through your own chattering teeth, your own wobbly knees and your own sense of righteousness.

It helps to see your enemy as a fellow soul lost in ignorance, lost in their own pond of misunderstood reflections. Imagine yourself as a seamless surface on the waters of life. And you are in relationships with ignorant forces as they appear on the surface of those waters. The pond you live on is indeed the planet Earth. Know that there are some frogs there, also toads and snakes. They are part of life and you are in it with them. So own the pond, the creatures and the beauty of it all put together. Own the opportunity and in your mind's eye find that needle, find that thread and stitch your way through all the things that come up in you. The movement through fear is indeed one heck of a dance. It may seem leagues away from revelation and the blissful realities called enlightenment. But from the very beginning to the end there is a thread.

There is a thread and at first that thread may be very quiet, but there is something in everyone. Even in the lowliest toad there is something eventually that can't be argued with. It's a movement towards that greater embodiment of truth in some small way. It may just be a begrudging sense of willingness to allow others to exist, but that is something. It's an acknowledgment of life even in the shadows, even if it is in the lowliest corner of your planet. And so, as aspirants behold yourself. In what you behold, see all whom you encounter and meet as a reflection of the self you are holding. If you are not looking for the sexy, heroic archetype, if you are looking under the surface of all myths and all images, you will find the power and aliveness of the central fire.

These are only words until you decide to mean business about this whole topic of individual awakening which has been manifesting for thousands of years. It appears in various ways through many books and many traditions. The power in this topic has been feared, and so there are many organizations and institutions that dampen it, hamper it and twist it up. The power in truth scares them. It creates games. You are in a world pond with all of these elements at work. And you have the challenge of moving through it in your mind so that you get to the truth. You need to check yourself in, throw your head on the table and see what is really inside. Don't be alarmed when you see the actual product. For all humans generally are alike, nine parts blame, three parts this and three parts that.

You are like most humans, wanting to have a good game. To put on a good show, you put some emotion in the mix. You care for your friends when you see their sense of fear. You want all of their lives to be just right. But to be engaged in that means you might not have to take care of your own fear and face the awful dilemma that is in your own emotional body. You have stuff hiding in the back closet, in the attic and the cellar, so you try to color how perception plays on the surface of the pond. But somewhere in your journey, if you are awake, you will know you are only victimizing yourself. You will see this from the miraculous perception on the spiritual hilltop. But you can't reside there because this teaching doesn't trump the necessity to handle daily life or hold perpetrators accountable. And you are obligated to maintain society's principles of conduct. Your own energy field, your mind-body, the aura therein and its dance is your corner of autonomy in the global pond. And with response from your spiritual heart you can affect it.

186

Sit yourself down deliberately intending to be attentive and stalwart about the fact that you have crap and you are willing to look at it. This is important because spiritual bliss is often misused. The drunken high from a spiritual group, a workshop, a healer or some other inspiration is often misused. That lift is energy wasted if misdirected. Its intended potential is to help you move through your shadow, to go into the cellar of your being. It should help you admit regret about your own conduct and mediocrity, sending healing light to that. But all too often it is directed at fixing others, society or the world. You'd do anything to avoid examining your own games and stuckness. So hold on to yourself fiercely through your own journey and shadow areas. Use spiritual energy to lift and evolve yourself. Spiritual energy is silly and sloppy when misused. Ego and the false sense of self is not often enough realized and seen through.

Be aware when you are inspired. When you feel that loving hit from others, realize the responsibility. Hold it close in your mind. Tend to it and allow it to shine light upon what is in the way of you being more of what you really are. Everyone here has similar tasks before them, to cultivate attentiveness to how wisdom needs to be used through the day. You need to have your own needle and thread to find the thread that runs through your day, your week and through your months. You must attend to the care of the body, care of the soul and care of your relationships in all of the multiple dimensions of your life. There are too many books about all the pieces of one's life. When you want to get to the heart of it, remember that all wisdom relates back to one wisdom. Remember that. Some people think these hard truths are funny. And they can be. Sarcastic commentary in the back corner is allowed. But think of how one gets locked in on a point trying to figure something out with limited human logic. Think of the weight that multiplies from being in that locked state. Consider the freedom available when that is surrendered.

The appearance of you as a dream character depends on the collapsing of an infinite field. For divinity to acquaint itself with human society, with its culture and function is a dramatic, huge collapse from the very illustrious fact that it is, you are infinite love. Trouble is born into that because there is such a likelihood of confusion, fear and feeling lost. Fear is useful for the tiger in the woods and for the host of biological critters on your planet. So understand the possibility of a positive relationship with fear and allow for it to be. But be watchful because it gets ramped up with human story. Confusion surfaces because there is plenty of intelligence available and used by dramatic souls. Humans love knowledge, they love emotion but do not like to face themselves. In the reflection of the pond we can grasp how lost most humans are.

We observe this in human culture. However, in seeking wisdom, you have some chance of seeing beyond this. So, yearn for the truth through whatever text or pathway works for you. Seeking this may be compelled by tragedy, exhaustion, strife or also by devotion to freedom. But it all takes an earnest alignment to see past perception in its play, to realize how it works. Anything that is slippery in nature is like the reflections in the pond. There is a profound capacity in humans to look into the myths of their own soul while sitting around the campfire or gazing at wind filling a sail. Your visions come from the poetic heart. They come from things like the direct contact with the wind filling the sail. What a profound tool for looking at the truth. The sea and wind are energy. The boat is a vessel in that energy and its captain needs to be in rapport with all of that.

At times, in order to survive another day, awesome attentiveness needs to be the focus for you as well. At times it is like you are in one universe and then another. A change of weather, a twist in a relationship or a phone call can change the very chemicals in your body. What are you doing to steer the sailboat? Are you being emotionally honest and vulnerable to life's essence? Are you asking for guidance? Contacting your intuitive nature through whatever way works for you is very necessary. It's like the sailor licking a finger to test the direction of the wind, for being lost can be quite dangerous. It can be all kinds of things, while on another level it is nothing. For, none of it is as real as you think it is. These two statements that Rhammah just spoke may seem to be contradictory. But, the answer to conflicting statements can only be found under the surface and between the layers. Your keenness for truth must see through all that manifests.

The kiss on the cheek from spiritual truth is undeniable. And the emergence of very real human dilemmas is equally undeniable. Discover what you really are for that infinite love knows the art and science of how to equally handle each situation. Dilemmas are affected by the art and science of perception. Just as there are situations which unarguably require logic, there are realms of your being that cannot be touched by logic. You may be grounded by reason, but don't be locked in by it. Really, how does anybody stand a chance when these elements are so in play? It is a deep question. And the aspirant needs audacity to trust that the intuitive self can handle it. And you can handle it. That fact is evidenced by the fact that you engage this wisdom.

This is the way infinite love gets through to your dimension. All of you are great lights. There are spots that can interrupt the light, but stay with the fact that you love the fire of scintillating truth in your belly. You love the possibility of revelation. And it comes in the form of a hero's journey as you walk through the wall of fear and make yourself vulnerable. Handing a piece of art to your brother or a bit of new wisdom to your sister is vulnerable. It is putting yourself on the table to be looked at, to allow for reactions to play out. It proves you are willing to put yourself out there with so little ego in a vulnerable way. Like, here is my heart and can you sense the fear in me as I offer it? Here is my humanity, given in this way to you. I have become an open book and I am trusting you.

In your little corner of humanity, you might protect and shelter yourselves, create a cocoon of support. But how great to be open to a family that doesn't agree with you. It's a whole pond of croaking frogs and you will become spiritually strong. Do you wish to be a pillar, to be aligned and stand tall as a great spiritual being? Then be trained here to handle it. Accept the forces and players in your life, as close to you as they are. Even better, do and say things that show what they choose is right for them. Love them that much, that you put down your own point of view. It is okay, because your point of view is just a particle that is lost in the fires of discovering what you are. And what you are originates before all perception. It is the primordial ooze that makes all perception possible. So what does any opinion matter? It is all infinite love.

Because of infinite love all five senses have manifested. And those five senses create a reflection upon the mind body organism in their dream. The greatest adventure is to move past that wall, that misconception of true self. We have suggested going into the closet and pretending to be a fan of the other team. Then you can come out of the closet and cheer for your team with gusto, with great conviction. But you won't be able to do it from our perception of truth until you can play the other side, until you know that what you are doing is a game in the world of form. That's how to play in a truth that indeed is quite uncommon. For it is quite common to say philosophically that "all the world is a stage." It is entirely another thing to live as if it is. It is uncommon to be the freedom in that truth and to show others that possibility.

We are giving you an assignment. To take responsibility for the actualization of your questions and your intentions. Stay with them like you have homework. Each acknowledgment is like a piston pumping energy. Each breakthrough is a golden nugget opening so your life releases more energy. That momentum creates revelation. It sets up a play for a great strident embodiment that is possible for all humans. You are peace for the world. You are peace for the world, and by being such the mind-body that you inhabit is being touched by that peace. Then the organism evolves its DNA. its patterning moves into the next dance of humanity. Human beings have been evolving throughout history by moving into potential this way. And you are actively engaging in that directive by embracing this teaching. We so acknowledge you. You are students. Speaking truth is a form of graduation. Rhammah bids thee adieu. Bless you all.

WHY NOT LET IT EVOLVE?

This life is like a candle flame dancing

Your identity evolves with the universe

It is all just one candle

just one flame

just one dance

Your being dances just like a flame

Relax into it and let it evolve

Discourse 5: Move Forward in Truth

What are you willing to go through? You may contemplate a capacity to know which can transform into an embodiment of knowingness. This is immersion into a truth where every question in your being is resolved. When the knowingness we are speaking about is relaxed into or leaped into, then one has dropped the world they know. In that capacity, all your questions become answers. Would you skip this dialogue with Rhammah for that awareness? Rhammah indeed will answer some of your questions, but we cannot do it without escorting you towards such a state of knowing. We might give you a taste, or prompt your being by giving it impulses or charges. We can offer glimpses to help convince your energetic self that you are speaking to and dancing with divine masters. Listen to those prompts and impulses.

In order to resolve the questions of this evening, listen to the core essence of your being. Allow the answers to be revealed in a very accidental fashion, like you are willing for the foundation of what you are to be affected. When you allow this, knowing gets birthed. It comes cracking through the very seams of your identity. When this happens, what you think and what is most dear to you can alter. Would you throw all that you are into the blender of truth and allow it to grow into a whole new way? In order to do this, there must be some contemplation about how your nature is accustomed to change. Your nature is similar to a caterpillar's which can be the larva, then nothing, and then a butterfly. Your nature is hypermorphic and radically transformative. It would astound you if you were to relax into it even a little.

So, we are here to prepare you for that. You are those who would say, "Yes indeed, even a hint of the truth would be good." You are those who would say, "I've had enough in this life to see the value and virtue of walking forward alongside those who have evolved in this dimension and moved on." Your world, whirling in vast space, is a world where the odds of creation, the likelihood of it giving birth to life is phenomenally enormous! And for life to evolve here to such a sophisticated level that the human has emerged, that is radically and more enormously improbable.

Know that the radical genius of life always seeks to move itself forward. It is the most astounding power, yet it can participate so gently that your world is a place where delicate flowers can blossom. The evidence of infinite grace, exquisite, docile and perfectly in balance, can be seen in the many life forms on this planet. And indeed, that enormous grace is also behind the apparent calamities of the universe, where worlds are swallowed up seemingly without care or even a thought. But divine purpose is in that, and is also evident in the worlds under this one, where the wretched exist in a choiceless muck of darkness.

In those worlds, a state of feeling tortured prevails. Those are places of choiceless blackness which seem to go on for all time with morbid agony. Souls get stuck in such circumstances by the gravity of their willful actions and destructive energies. But do understand, for the sense of choice to exist in some realms, there must be realms that are choiceless. They sit alongside and create each other so that darkness can evolve into choice. What does it take for one to evolve up out of those places? It is quite difficult. So, take care that you do not get pulled by your choices back into those painful lessons.

Here on Earth you have vicious life forms with sharp teeth that eat other life forms in their normal behavior. That is part of the grace of Infinity existing on this planet as the full range of experience. It should be honored as part of the full scale of development. But it can be perplexing for you to sense your place in this spectrum. You struggle to understand why you cannot get full relief or full cure from its harsh norms. In the history of this planet, there were many forms of human, like Hominid, Neanderthal, Homo Sapiens and Homo Sapiens-Sapiens. In this progression, each vessel was able to contemplate bigger truths, nobler ways. They evolved slowly, but an acceleration is now upon you to radically evolve very quickly as compared to any time or place in history.

There is an apex of forces coming together to play out in you. The upheaval that goes with this dynamic time is necessary. It is like a baby growing teeth. You must talk to the baby and say, "The discomfort is so worth it, for you will chew on corn, pumpkin pie and potatoes. You will have a new world of experiences and possibilities. Pained gums are so worth it my little one. It is so right, so take it in and adapt." You are all being prepared for a radical awakening. And there is often some anguish with such growth. It occurs because your human vessel is evolving and needs to be prepared. Forerunners like yourselves need to be willing to go through the discomfort it can take to be prepared, to be hardened to handle what you will wrestle with. You are courting a revelation, hearing of truths which you may be troubled by. Essentially, your cranium is being rewired for an expanded understanding.

Humans often wonder how two things can be true at the same time. We often tell you that this world is an illusion, and that this world is also completely real. You ask how can both of these can be true? We have searched many historical philosophies looking for ways to prepare entities for such grand paradoxes. But there is no exact precedent. In spite of that, we press forward, preparing you for that noble moment where the questions are handled by the knowingness which emotes. This knowing state is alive. It will take you to the apex of the capacity for this world. It can also take you beyond it if you hold true to the fact that all fear is illusion. All fear is illusion! That very phrase will guide you through the many turns of a life if you apply it consistently.

In the evolution that we are directing you towards, illusion takes over less often. And the truth that it is all an illusion will increase. Gradually, you will see through the veils offered by the layers of comfort and entropy. (Entropy means a collapsing or a tendency toward disorder. It can also refer to energy breaking down and not being able to be utilized or drawn upon). Your entropy is intertwined and interlocked with the entropy, the density of humanity. Its comforts have been perfected by humans, and they are not so helpful. There are ways of thinking that hold this entropy in place. These unhelpful ways of thinking get held in place by many entities who are not so helpful. Know that many of the beings who foster this entropy don't inhabit human bodies. They are floaters, connected to your planet, who hold in place the space of entropy for those who are in bodies and also those out of body. It is how the illusion prevails and is promoted.

The construct of life as you know it is held together by humanly interpreted systems of perception and structure. Such systems in density are like hampering shackles. But they are also the glue that sticks humanity together. They are agreements which allow you to be able to function and interact with each other. In order for relationships to play out in your societies you need these agreements, as illusory as they are. They make it convenient, possible, and are also not always helpful in the evolution towards the truth of your being. You are the ones who must walk this razor edge of living as you go into your advancement. And for we masters from forever to speak to you as humans, we must partially embrace the same illusions of your dimension and world. Of course, this is paradoxical to the human mind. So, learn to live with that paradox.

Do you know there is an actual gravity to your delusion? It has a pull, like a candy bar pulls on a sugar addict's mind, like the

196

thought of chocolate whets your desire. It works like a black hole which draws all toward it. The dance with sugar, for example, over a period of time creates a habitual agony which is not helpful to the body or mind. A more helpful awareness needs to enter the orbit of the conscious mind. An awakening entity will start to feel a new pull, drawn by a helpful gravity that is more sustaining. Eventually this new pull must win out or there will be health issues. There are many layers of gravity in the ways your being operates. The ultimate antidote for this pull of gravity is for a human to embrace the knowing that it is all an illusion. It is not so real as it seems.

One of the great forces pulling in the opposite direction is fear. The apparent reality of your dimension fits together perfectly and serves to fosters fear. It includes the subtle games of control, and even your rebellious sarcasm and intimidation which relies on fear and illusion. Fear resides in its grandest forms on your planet. It is bound by the presumption that all of this is real. And that presumption is bound tightly to your entire identity. The idea of your physical form being real traps you. If that can be dismissed, the whole house of cards collapses. Are you actually willing to do that work, knowing that your metaphorical gums might hurt so badly? There are those who have done such preparation. They have helped humans move into a greater capacity to embody the energy of great truth. They have walked forward in spite of the stretching and adjustment this requires.

You are walking forward, all of you, into what Rhammah is teaching. Some part of you knows of the horror of choicelessness that exists in the dark realms. You are aware of the ignorance and wretchedness in the thick quagmire of such lower worlds, for you all have cellular memory of this in your being. And because of this, an invitation to embrace these teachings plays through you on some level. It is the back and forth action in your being. But because you seek it, a movement forward to greater truth will ultimately prevail, even though at present there is still that back and forth. Those wobbles can be your yearning for certain comforts from the darkness, like chocolate three times a day, alcohol every evening, computer games or perhaps some drug. There are places in your psyches that justify those addictions.

Most humans are convinced that such diversions work. And that is okay. Do you remember the lesson of looking in the mirror with love for yourself? Bring presents to yourself with great love. Why not also have a conversation in front of the mirror. It would go like this, "I've seen you live nobly and truthfully. I've seen you charm your friends and be kind to your children. There are all these good things about you. I also love you, even the sugar coated, gaming, stuffy parts of you. I love that you are willing to hear these difficult lessons and embrace what you are able. I am so happy to be with you, oh ego in the mirror. I can see where you are going. You are moving towards a greater place. And in spite of the difficulties, you continue walking uphill. I value that about you."

Such evolving is not easy. But when you see the greater picture it becomes easier. Of course, you would grow teeth so that you could eat corn. Of course, you would strive to walk forward and move out of the gaming ways of humanity that you wrestle with. Say to yourself, "I will reach below those impulses and look into the heart of my being. I will come forth with greater alignment and take on the growing pains that allow for the energy to be embodied in this form." This is no small offering to yourself, or to your friends, or to humanity. It is a grand marching forward into an embodiment, a way which knows that there is only the highest good to be done. Accept that this world and its choices are sandwiched between the worlds of black choicelessness and the harmonious worlds you will evolve into.

Ironically, there is actually a sense of choicelessness in this evolutionary direction we are encouraging you towards. It works like this. Before thought, there is the knowing that all which moves is grace itself. The highest good is simply known innately from the belly of the universe. And that highest good is done. That is all that you will know when you graduate. It will be blissfully choiceless grace, drunk with itself. It is eternal, infinite, all powerful, exquisite awareness. In your realm, you are free to enjoy the sense of apparent choice. It is structured that way to assist you in lessons. To help you discover and comprehend a truth which can function fully while being held in an illusory construct that seems true and real.

To be what is termed transcendent, both hands need to be holding the fabric of this dimension, this apparent world of "me identity." When both hands knowingly hold this fabric and agree to be with it, that is how the loving of it gets emoted. For that staying capacity of love to flow forth from you, you need to know simultaneously that this is not real, but it also functions as real. In so doing, you hold your own babe in your arms with all your might. With all of your tenderness, you grab her on the cheek realizing this little, delightful illusion is showing you the truth. You become the embodiment of a greater truth that the universe and all that is behind it is so eternally mysterious. Within and because of this mystery, you have appeared. This is indeed a miracle that makes one dizzy. It is a miracle made none-the-less because you know it isn't fundamentally real.

All of this is happening as you have relaxed towards this tasty fruit, the truth of knowing. You have become its very nectar, its very quality. It has come to life in you, and it will be starkly true. You will see that many who do not know this truth are lost in mean and very wretched ways. For those who know, they know how exquisitely perfect it is that all of this is dancing on the head of a pin in an unbelievably vast cosmos. It is barely real, this radically subjective arena with layers of light dancing as layers of appearance. With advancing knowledge, the spectrum of understanding available in human experience is evolving and growing. That is why some humans are now ready for this wisdom. Your world's movement, its dance of life is rather like a flame on a candle. The whole experience of human life is dancing, flickering, keeping most humans captive.

Those who are more thoughtful, they are holding a space on this planet. So, delve into and hold your intellect like a baby. When it hurts, talk to it about sore gums and corn. Your intellect is going through growing pains. By intention, your being is in a constant state of challenge. It has been given the perfect circumstances for what it needs to grow. All babes go through teething. And most humans take on things like egotistical husbands, assertive wives, testy children, pesky pets, physical challenges and trying occupations. You throw yourself into the fray of human experience. It is a game, for somehow you are aligned to find your way back to Source, even though it seems impossible not to stay lost in the brilliant illusion. You have thrown yourself into it knowing you would find your way out.

This planet is a grand school, a hall of mirrors and a tricky quagmire generated and held up in front of you. Your mind is glued upon it by devices like acquisition, belief, opinions, self-importance and fear. You can say, "I dismiss this, for all attachment and fear is illusion. I move forward into truth. I thank all that is occurring in my life, for it resonates within me that this is all perfectly right as it is." Focus on such reminders and your identity will evolve with the universe. It is all one candle, all one flame just dancing. Why not walk into all fears knowing that they are just appearances? Evolution gets accelerated, kick started, and you will be amazed before you are one step in. You will be even more amazed, because the revelations will come forth from your own being.

Go into your own being fearlessly, turning over stones in the story about your childhood, your parents and your encounters. It is good to turn over those stones and see how feelings and agreements were put together. For your story is stitched mysteriously within the fabric of the illusion. There is a sense in a master that he or she is smiling into the darkness. So, smile into your own darkness, into that which scares you the most. Confront that which might be revealed, which might warn off the social selves you wish to emulate or project. A master is gentle with all of that. You are playing with life like a child would play with clay. You play in these meaty, juicy areas of your mind and your memory. And this rich play of consciousness occurs in self-made vessels, composed of divine qualities and also the thicker, darker ignorance.

Look upon your past entanglements as the best that you could do at the time. Those entanglements were promoted and held together by the entropy of humanity. Your many agreements, which are often rooted in innocent misunderstandings, have gravitational pull. They are holding you in limitation. There are layers and layers within the individual souls in the environment that you are witnessing. Each one of you are also part of a collective of beings. Some collectives are more intimate while others are more broad. But, in the many matrixes of energy, you are connected to all beings and all that is. When you move forward into truth, all of these facts light up. You shake the Earth with even a subtle shift of your attention. For this is all an illusion, and it is the lack of knowledge thereof that drives wretchedness. The chemistry of this dance is alive with dichotomy. It's flame burns within you regardless, so relax about it.

We have presented you with a teaching that shifts between two truths. Everything is real, and everything is not. When you embrace that, you go into the illusion while relaxing out of it. Knowing that all fear is illusion, you are able to relax into your own true space. Ask the core of you being to organize your consciousness and make room for this dichotomy. Let it reveal the truth as a shimmering, ever evolving light emanating from you. In doing so, all of the answers will be handled by your own nature. You will be lifted above your own minds. You will see that your minds are works of art, part of the grace that is the illusory universe and the way it dances like the flame. Create a discussion about this. Speak of what you are becoming and what pains you are glad to go through. Rhammah bids thee adieu great masters. Indeed.

PART FIVE

WISDOM

LET US SET SAIL ON A SPIRITUAL QUEST

Let us be willing to:

set our sails on a course, put our rudders in the water

risk our "life as we know it," to shake and be shaken up

be put to the test, to be put up against a hot fire

find our way peacefully through the waters that are presented

see all matters as small, face them like a gentle giant

steer with the rudder of knowing

smile from inside, as we also smile into another

Let us be willing to know the winds of the divine

are filling our sails with grace and power

to stay the course,

as we set sail on a spiritual quest

Discourse 1: Going Beyond Limited Beliefs

Learning about life, truth, wisdom and the whole works is an important and gratifying human activity. It is quite noble to study the processes, both small and large, that lead towards wisdom. So, let us set our sails on a course and put our rudders in the water. When a sailor sets out upon the sea there is great uncertainty. This was especially true in days gone by. Those who set sail were very courageous, willing to face the great risk. Here, we are not talking about a risk to your physical life if you pursue the adventure of wisdom. We are talking about the risk to your "life as you know it." In this effort you will shake and be shaken up. What you hold dear will be put to the test. It will be put up against a hot fire.

So, we ask you this question. Will the thinking processes you call your beliefs last in the hot fires which are the tests of wisdom? With this metaphor of a boat, you can imagine going across an ocean. You've seen images of ships riding on mountainous waves as treacherous as a volcano. To be a sailor on such a quest is no small matter. With determination you need to put your rudder in the water and set your sail for a spiritual quest. Do not settle for a limited belief or a cool concept. Put your whole being up against the test. Measure it against what you truly are in your core and live in your knowing. Living in knowing is like having your rudder in the water.

When a person is rudderless and unsure of themselves, it is more likely for them to be converted by one philosophy or another. Persuasive people may say to an uncertain person, "Oh, she looks wobbly, we ought to get ahold of her. We ought to show her the truth and show her the way that we follow." This is how it works. So, own your own field and say, "I will steer my boat to knowing. I will be the example of one who is in the know, one who realizes that the truth is an abiding absolute. This is in the core of my being and I choose to inhabit that." In the strength of that mindset, you are assured and confident. You are teaching through your field, touching all through who you are.

To hold a posture like this is to be unavailable for conversion to more limited beliefs. If approached you can simply respond, "Ah, what a fantastic idea. That is a grand metaphysical concept. The teachings of Jesus, what a grand story, what a grand parable." When you smile from the belly of your being and inhabit this vessel as a confident spirit, then Jesus is simply your brother, Mary is simply your sister and they inhabit what you also are as Divine Source manifested. I invite you into this confidence now. You can pray for it. You can meditate to be on your way to it. You can do all sorts of things or you can just embrace it directly.

I want you to know that the uncertainty in you, the wobbliness, confusion, lack of confidence, lack of resolve and especially the fear can all be dismissed. Declare, "From the Lord of My Being, I smile like a radiant sun. Right here as I sit on this stump my heart is fire, and I live in the highest knowing now." You can affirm this resolve with eyes open or with eyes closed. You can do it driving down the street or washing your dishes.

This revelation of your being is always completely available to you in every moment. But that may set you up, because your husband forgot to park the car in the driveway when you asked him to. Or your neighbor who does not shovel his driveway or his sidewalk or fix his house irritates you. Those dilemmas in your own self are the twenty-foot mountainous wave. You say, "How dare he, how dare she?" And suddenly the resolve to be a brilliant smile for the universe, for humanity, for your neighbor, for your partner is gone.

Are we setting you up for an easy task? Hardly, but it is simple and that is what makes it notable and worthwhile. The waves in your own being rock you and fill your brain from ear to ear with the mantra of why me. "Why does this have to happen to me," you ask? But I ask, "Have you set your sail on this course, put your rudder in that water? How many people do?" There is so much collective human affirmation to stay in the loop of your mindset. Human convention supports many limited beliefs and allows them to wreak havoc on your life because there is not yet enough dedication to the elevated, expanded concepts. Think like this, "I am on course to be the Lord of My Being through every bit of water that gets thrown in my face by my own self." Ask yourself, "What is really of my own self?" We tell you that all of it is, all of creation is you. Try that one on for size. You will not like it. Or, I should say your own ego will not like it at all.

What are your minds muttering regarding this? Are they saying, "I don't know if I like this? I don't know if I want this philosophy? Maybe he's right, but maybe he's not." All that flip flopping in your being is good stuff for those who would like to convert you. Conversion is not the Rhammah Masters' agenda. Do we want you to study this wisdom? It would be alright if you do. You might find the beautiful occurrence of a person awakening enough to consider this wisdom. You may find your own way by discovering which boat you like, which rudder you need and what course you will take. But all paths are really the same when you understand that truth is available within you. It is so abiding that it will be more attractive than anything outside of this deep inner source.

With that said, let's go back to how much of your crap comes from inhabiting your human body with its limited perceptions. How great is the emptiness inside when you have a pattern of needing everything to be right, of needing all the ducks to be in a row so completely? If you could feel that emptiness, really feel the dryness and the awesome weight of that physical identity's core patterns, a great shift might occur. This emptiness holds you in a place of misery for so many hours in a day. Don't you want to have a radical breakthrough? Make your measure of success and happiness be the degree to which you can be in a joyous space and find your way peacefully through the waters that present each day.

You might say, "This trip with my husband in the nursing home and all that it brings me, what a good practice. It has been so useful and interesting." That is the sound and song of a master. "This dance with cancer, being in and out of the hospital with these health issues, what an interesting opportunity. It is all happening for me and now I know more about who I really am. I know what the most permanent parts of me are and I'm in touch with the infinite self, with the eternity that I am. What an interesting play. I am being taught so perfectly well by life." A master will look at situations in this way. A being striving for awakening will work at embracing such viewpoints.

So, what of your days ahead? Have you put your boat into the water, set sail with the rudder in deep and allowed for messy waters to be completely okay? Can you honestly say, "Whatever is to be, let it hit me? What I really want is to be head on with each challenge." When you're hit with a large wave, you do not want to be mushy. You want to be head on so you survive it. Be like that in the waters of life and face onslaughts completely, strategically knowing that what's in you can take whatever is coming. Think, "I will concern myself with arriving skilled and with a big smile into the storm. I will take it head on for what is in me is that strong. It is infinite."

Those who burn bridges, those who have messy relationships, do they create their own waters? There are waters that you humans are so sure you did not create. But step back and think about it. You all inhabit bodies. You live on a planet that has had one uncertainty after another through all its history. And forever you have all been worried about the end of the world. This collective conundrum is what you signed up for. You are here for this great adventure, so bring it on. Normal human rough spots are small challenges compared to actually being touched by the light and existing next to what Allness really is. You would not be the same if even one fingertip touched that power source. You would be taken apart for a hundred years at least, unable to use your mind because the bliss of Total Divinity is so awesome. Your cares would seem so futile in the beauty of its truth.

Can you embark on measuring your moments against that? Does that feel true or seem available? Do you believe those who came to testify to such a truth, even if a religion was made after their sojourn? Of course there are arguments and various presumptions about a figure like Jesus. That will go on forever. But who of the light has not been misrepresented amongst humanity? And how could they be completely represented considering your human limitations? All your questions and confusion which fuel fervent study and weeks and months and years of questioning, that is an example of what you should relax. Face it head on, but also be unconcerned. What we are offering is an invitation to something other than trying to know the truth with intellectual processes.

It is natural for your intellect to wonder if channeled teachings can be trusted. But in a world of beings with limited perception and active egos, do you really know where any of your wisdom originated from? There are those who might benefit from contact with a god that represents them and is not lost in conditioned human mindsets. I am Rhammah. I am not a human. I am god as much as you are. This Host has moved aside enough for me to touch down and share time and energy with you. This allows me to inhabit this moment to assist you in your quest for understanding the true self. I represent the unadulterated truth of what Divine Source really is. We present this truth with human words and concepts that attempt to describe the unfathomable awesomeness of Supreme Allness. And, hopefully the god which is in you is enticed to go for it.

So, see all human matters as small and face them like a gentle giant. Care about being exquisitely skillful with each detail of your life. Be prayerful and meditative about each action, because you are this Lordliness. What is in you is absolutely grand, but you are not convinced of it, so you take up these teachings. Let us inspire you to do some work and try to get past yourself. Let's shock you with a transmission that sends you into contemplation of your eternal self. Find it right now, for in every detail of this experience there is evidence of your divinity. You are that which is alive and can speculate about the concerns of this body and its intellect. You can decide what to know, to ponder what to teach and what not to teach, what to join and what not to join.

Think about this. You can be convinced to inhabit this body with great love, with great "yes" energy. Your bodies are vessels for magnificent beings, so be aware with every tactile experience from your butt on the cushion and your toes on the floor to the quality that is your hair. Being with everything completely is the practice of yes and evidence of your divinity. This is it! So, go nowhere else. Understand that by saying yes from your heart and from the core of your being radiant divine love turns up. It turns up with each yes. You are blessing this room, all of these neighbors and this whole community at each moment when you inhabit this divine experience. In the most loving, graceful way you are lifting the world. So, join in that directive. Do it in whatever way works for you in your life.

There are so many things to learn in your human arena that are esoteric. You can pick up the cards, learn the numbers, go into past lives and traditions, have this teacher, and another teacher, and another. It goes on and on. Is that all wrong? No, not at all. Perhaps you like being with your friends on the other side, hearing them talk and feeling their presence. Is that wrong? Not at all, just as it isn't wrong to learn about your astrological chart and see where all the planets lived when you were born. None of these are wrong, but what occurs with these engagements is a posture of being convinced that the truth lives in a segmented space, in a process of many things. When you discover the Lord of Your Being it all changes. It merges into oneness. All of it is the possible expression of that which is available in you right now.

You do need to be aware that knowing is an alone process. There have been those who were able to stomach themselves enough, stomach the smell of their own crap enough to keep moving forward through it. For those who are able to do that, a sense of humor is helpful. It is imperative to have a light-hearted resolve about the journey. Can you insist that this world you've come into, this body and situation you've come into is an important journey which is like a school? And in order to graduate a good sense of humor is necessary. You must be able to laugh off your troubles and find the silver lining in the most difficult situations. Bite down on that requirement. Make sure you are with it and tread the waters of your troubles right to the beach of this destiny of awakening.

So, allow for this world to have its schools of thoughts and beliefs. On this adventure, be willing to get loosened from the limited schools you've given your soul to. Then you will become one who thinks for yourself instead of having them think for you. Some of you have been escorted to fit into one box or the other. You have been pressured and you've been convinced in various ways. This is why it is an awesome turning in one's life to hear about taking a stand and walking like a master, living like a master. When you know about the light of your Source which you might touch with a finger or feel as closely as a hair on your head, you cannot be unmoved. And that creates a situation where you will have to check in your ego. To walk this truth without ego or hypocrisy, your life must emulate the values of the highest expression.

So, you can explore what interrupts resolve by resetting what resolve is all about. Experience your surroundings and bring the Lord of Your Being on board. It is a radiant sun of divinity creating a space of infinite love. Everything that challenges that space is your teacher because it shows you what you have running. You may hear a voice say, "Ah, I need you to like this or that for the sake of others." That is the ego. It creates huge waves in many humans. Ego may say, "I need to be heard. I need my spirituality to be acknowledged by others." That's another one, and it goes on and on and on imagining how you can benefit from this posture or that action. But the experience of the Lord of Your Being gives you clarity to set the sails and drop the rudder. When you are leveled by this truth, the wave comes and you know you are going to face it, move through it and let it pass over you.

Find your own approach to life that comes from your spiritual heart. Find your approach and it will start to look like, "How can I be grateful for my husband? How can I be grateful for my wife? How can I be grateful for my father and my mother and for all this world and all that it is?" When you have tasted the light, you are concerned about the rubbish your own self can produce. Face everything from a place that connects to the Lord of Your Being. You are bigger than any problem, yet you can also be with it in a unique way. It is as if you are the gentlest giant with the most delicate, skillful hands. You are the most sensitive soul with a responsiveness, a dedication to being an example of divine love. This concern helps you to process yourself in a way that each problem is dismissed.

This higher energy has the quality of "everything is right." Everything is transformed and seen in a new way. Sadness becomes so right, so harmonious. Anger becomes so right because it is accepted. That is stage one. Most of you are working on that. Stage two includes the human emotion. The divinity which inhabits the body creates an emoting process where powerful, blissful chemicals can run through the body. There is less wobbliness and a smile hits the cheeks in an effortless way. Your body-mind says, "I am infinite love. That is what matters, I am infinite love. That is what matters." To hear these teachings out of curiosity is not wrong. To come to them again and again out of curiosity is not wrong. It is not wrong to miss the boat time and time again. It is just off the mark. It's not the best focus to take on this teaching with only half your heart.

So, when will you be ready to take this teaching on? It is okay to put your toes in the water of divinity. It is a great start. But why not see what it is like to wash it up on your arms and your shoulders and feel its strength and its calming power. Allow it to play through all of your being. When you do that you will have emoting energy with the whole field of love that you are. When you are with your friends, when you are walking down the hall, when you are driving down the street be concerned with whether or not your energy is lifting others. Why not do that? Don't be pushy or super smiley. Be so quiet and subtle but smile big in your energy, for divinity is at your feet. It is to the left and to the right and far below. It is in your breath and in every cell of your body. Experiment with how quietly you can smile into another.

You could put on a crazy smile or squeeze someone's cheek. You could grab them in a big hug or laugh till they laugh with you. But your world is quite complex and you have social norms and boundaries for what people are ready for and not ready for. So, go forward quietly without doing anything obvious. Just smile from inside. Let the God of Your Being smile out into the room in a way that each being is profoundly touched. Be so quiet that you are laughing with them, yet there is nothing obvious going on. In your mind, be with them like your own beloved child and smile radiantly. In the subtly of this embrace know you are giving. Smile into those who give you a bitter taste, who trouble you. What is in them is also of divinity. Touch that with your mind's eye and smile right through yourself. Take all that you think of them, even the troubled part and know there is only God.

Say, "I choose to give this great vibration to all, across the board equally." Dedicate yourself to this as the winds of the divine fill your sails, giving you the grace and power necessary to be on course. Steer with the rudder of knowing, dismissing pedantic intellectual processes, dismissing religious conjecture and schools of thought, teachers and teachings. Dismiss enough so that you can be on course to the pure godly self which radiates in knowing. That is an alignment with the original you. Stand as tall as king and as sure as the most humble sage who lives under a bridge. Be free of the dance of separate human identity while being in it completely.

Sit as eternity would sit for a millennium and be resolved to dismiss all stories about your separate self-identification. Be on course to know the unshakable presence of your original consciousness. A troubled life is a gift which can show you the misery of your "me consciousness" which is so non-useful. Wear that sucker out or choose this alignment now. Say, "I am this Lordly Way." I am Infinite Love." It is time to be completely aligned, unshakably resolved. You can claim it now. Rhammah is blessed by you. You have picked up the phone and we are listening. We have come in grand fashion. We would like you to all chant Om as we leave. Greet the Host with that beautiful healing sound.

WISDOM

This vessel is an instrument

Animated in one creative source, playing out in creation

Allow the thunder of life to play now

Intimate, authentic, alive, a note playing a cord for its own sake

A magical moment in the great wisdom of spontaneous self

Embrace your life

So guarded and so kingly that you do not need soldiers

So rich, that you do not need ornaments

So worthy, you do not need material or the good fortune of others

So right, no one needs to agree

So right, you do not need to speak

Immense power is quite natural

Go into the Song of Commitment to Wisdom

Discourse 2: Being the Song of What Is Real

Like a violin, a cello or a guitar, this vessel is an instrument. Honoring its song, letting it loose through the throat honors the instrument and its capacity to play. There are wisdoms we must salute with a thousand hands, wisdoms of creativity and of being in touch with the muse, singing, playing, living joyously. All of you have played in the wisdom of my song. There are those of you who have flowered and blossomed in the expression of self more than others. Reflect on the wind in the belly, the wind that fills your chest. It has the capacity to spell and thunder out sound as well as breath through the vessel. If you are gripping on spoken words you may fail to hear the song. Or you might be grasping for answers, and for that reason you will not hear the song.

We speak of your vessel's creativity and its creation. For all vessels are animated by the one creative source playing in creation. And you have played in honor of your creativity. There are those who come to Rhammah asking which instrument to play. They are the individuals who stay stuck. They ask, "Which instrument do I play Rhammah? Is there a right one to play?" Even if I answer their questions from the perspective of big knowing, it goes over their heads and they stay stuck in wondering which specific instrument to play. In truth, it doesn't matter. When one is driven to know the song that is in their core, they will jump into the fray. They will play whatever their hands are able to grasp. They will take it and grow with it no matter what is available.

In all your human history from its earliest, earliest days there have been creative moments. They all are expressions of the capacities of that moment. And it is always a most excellent moment. Suppose there are two sticks that you can beat together. That is the instrument of the moment. You have a voice, feet to stomp and the power to thump your chest. That is your inheritance, your current capacity. Will you say yes to it? Will you allow that thunder of life to play? For what use is it to wonder what will come? There are the instruments of the moment and the divinity that animates your form. The spontaneity of a child is the song you miss when you want to know what will happen tomorrow or how you will it be funded. You take the spirit that is alive and package it, pumping it out, creating a thing and losing the imminent vitality.

We do salute all the teachings of how to do your dreams. We honor all the wisdoms from your whole life, all that has nourished you. So, bring it here now. Put it in front of you and look at your whole lifetime's collection. There are those of you who have passed the test and said, "I will take my voice forth, I will be that song." Wisdom goes on a card that says, "Here I am, here I am." You are playing your song, indeed. and that wisdom we salute with a thousand hands. But now, if you've connected with this wisdom you have a whole new set of problems. A new batch of things to deal with if you are ready for this new wave.

Understand that there are so many belief systems and many are compromised. What crystallizes and forms around any established wisdom is a finality, a rigidity. Ideas are captured and put into stasis. That which is alive gets put into dogma and is encapsulated. It is now an object for your mind, and you are missing out on the intimate, authentic alive note playing its cord for its own sake without a thought of tomorrow. We are speaking of authenticity that is like a child's elation when there is only this magical moment in the now. In such moments agendas, dreams, securing, fretting about the future are absent, replaced by what is real. For what manifests is a distant flicker on the horizon when you are in the great wisdom of the spontaneous self. That is infinite wisdom, so how do you squish it to the size of a peanut? You worry that such spontaneous creativity might not become what you think it could. But know that if it dies, it was all that was needed. A day was all that was needed. A great creation or a castle in the sandbox, both are so right for something to flower forth many days or many years from that moment.

You wonder why students come and don't return? We do salute what you bring with a thousand hands. But we then attempt to wash it away. This is because much that is precious to you is now in the way of your awakening. What you have learned with your years is now obsolete. It's a layer of an onion to be dumped and peeled away for the new vista. We just exhaled sound to counteract the static sitting on your shoulders. We aim to stun the mind so that what is real can sit with you. In the after-wake of this expelling of sound, your worldly concerns are so distant from your godliness. Those concerns are small issues compared to the bigness. We bring what is grand, you are stunned for an instant and then the noise of all your issues comes right back. So, embrace the noise for it is not a problem. It cannot squish the grandness that you truly are.

In this human experience, every happy-go-lucky, creative, jumpy critter that you've ever met is having a party of some sort. The objects and creatures of your life are your toys in the playground. So, which toy do you play with first? It is wise to be guarded and so kingly that you do not need soldiers, so rich that you do not need ornaments, so worthy you do not need the material, the good fortune or praise from others. Be so right no one needs to agree with you and so right you do not need to speak. Latch onto the song that is alive and real. Find what is natural and know that immense power is quite natural. You wonder what that looks like, how it behaves? All the answers that your mind gives must be blown to the wind or you lose what's real again.

When fears rumble through your body, your human mind looks for the answer because all that you care about is at stake. Instead, ask yourself to go to the song of what is real with more commitment than ever before. Take a break from intellectual constructs and merge with authenticity in the most real sublime way. There is so much value, so much merit and so much traction in being grateful for the tests that come to your being. Great souls from many dimensions come to this third dimension for such tests. You have earned them so step right up. Face the earthquake, the auto accident or the incurable disease and look into your soul to the place before all answers, before all problems and creative pulses. Be tested, you've earned it and you are loved so greatly.

In billions of years of evolution, creation has created a planet spinning around the sun that has life on it. The pulse behind that is awesome complexity. Your Earth is wonderful, haunting, spirit crunching and uplifting, for you are in school. Many of your brothers and sisters are taking tests that you won't have to. So, how do you lift the planet's energy? You thank your brothers and sisters. You thank them and honor their wisdom as an infinite being born to take on amazing misfortunes. They are only a small sliver of all humans on your planet who have gone through similar or worse. There are good days and many that have been far worse. Therefore, know what is behind all of life. What existed before everything has so much love and power. And that is where you can find ultimate peace about all your imagined impasses.

Many souls are more likely to pass the bigger tests than you if you are in a happy-go-lucky lifetime. But bask in the sun of an easy lifetime if it is there for you. We are not saying you should call misfortunes upon yourselves. Don't drop everything and go into the desert forgetting your food and water. Just remember your brothers and sisters, thanking the place in them which has chosen to take this on. That provides an energetic boost for what is real from the home of the masters which is also where you come from. When Rhammah answers your questions and they go over your head, think of those who are in their tests. Hold their souls in your mind and say, "Look, you need to see where home is. You are forced into your heart of hearts for there is no place to go other than that. You are kissed with the greatest wisdom. Thank you, my brother, my sister." As you do that it is also true for you, for you are all in your own tests.

As you pluck knowledge from the tree of life there is the big unknown. So know that a thousand hands of love are upon you in the human process. You endure the aching, the hardness and the en-tangling. There is all of that and while the stiffness, the worry, the future concerns and turbulent concepts of your minds are allowed to be, there is also the soupy, everywhere quality of energy. Rhammah salutes all that you've put together and you should salute it too. Sa-lute it and then blow it to the wind, for there is only energy. A deep breath falls naturally into the belly when there is only energy. In the thousand hands from the great masters everywhere, there is only en-ergy. When the reality of all is known, a great weight falls off the shoulders and only spontaneous, alive, authentic and uncontrived energy is left.

So, why doesn't this make sense to your human minds? It's be-cause we are sharing a more expanded reality than has ever been shared. Ours is a testimonial to a realm that was spoken of in books from ancient times and is still pertinent. We add to that. You have many chapters of your life like the breakthroughs. You think, "I fi-nally got what I want. I have answers and these answers work, they are practical. I like how it's working." But how long does that sus-tain you, for a day, a week, a year or five? Then comes the break-down of that flow and you are in the ebb of the cycle. You scurry about in a frantic dance to make it all right again. For under the breakthrough there was still the aching, hungry human. That same aching was underneath the frantic energy when the flow of resources, of vitality and capacity ended.

Rhammah is speaking about how you get blown out of the water. Your permeating reality under the ups and downs of life is the concern for a self and a dream that is far less real than you can possibly imagine. To persist with our wisdom, means you have probably tried all of the answers that might seem to work. You thought this worked or that worked, but still there was the aching, hungry soul who was worried the flow might not last. When that is tossed away, one can tend to a vision that emanates from joy. It rises from spontaneity and power and it can finally be fully alive. I am Rhammah. Rhammah bids thee adieu. We will bring Novo. The energy work continues.

(*Novo enters the Host*) What is wanted is reality. When it appears, it appears. What is natural in you has always been there. We turn what you see upside down in such a way that you no longer see it with worry and concern. You see with the bigness of Source which is alive with power that is true. You who are awash with pain, allow what Rhammah says to be revealed in its own way in you. Make way for what is needed for you at this minute. There are questions, swarming on top of a big belly of knowing that is so real to you. Be with all that you are. Include the concept that it is Oneness. Then there will be no fight. You are faced with the fight in you. Your eyes see it out there. So, take it in, own it. It is all you.

The dance of a healer is a dance. That is all. When you know this, you will feel so free. The toughest souls on your journey, thank them for the lessons they bring to you. Complete a phase and move forward. When it is seen differently than learning, the wind will be at your back. While all is well, there is still the life lived with both hands committed to your day. So, allow this dream to play itself out, allow. See a path through a whole wave of your journey as a spiritual being that is getting more real. I am right here with you. What is in you is in me. When you greet another, look into their eyes and relax into how big you are. To beat the drum of what you really are, all that you know must be tossed aside for that authenticity.

When you greet your friends, do not do so as a healer, or as a helper, or as a nice person, bring it all. So, how would you sing? There is the easy joy of a special moment, your day in the sun. And there is also the joy that sees even the hardships with unswerving love for all that appears. Smile through it all and stay steady with what is alive in you while life plays out. We bid thee adieu. School is in session.

WHAT IS A SILENT GENERATOR OF ENERGY?

It is a result of looking into oneself

Into one's internal awesome knowing

The capacity for all experiences

It is inquiry about your good sense

The genius of life

The pure source energy of your being

For the capacity to pump energy from forever into the world

Is in the ordinary blessings you give

In recognizing that nothing is happening

In knowing within that everything is happening

So, recognize self as a silent generator of energy

Discourse 3: Non-Phenomenal, Non-Dimensional Self

Tend to yourselves honestly and you are more likely to approach yourself appropriately. It is similar to how you might approach the day appropriately by getting a sense of the weather patterns for that day. It is also good to know the season and the patterns of the environment you are in. Like that, when you find the capacity to be with yourself honestly, it's as if you can touch your own pulse. Then you stay with it and watch it, monitoring and discovering the magnificent fact that you are eternal, that you are of eternity. By discovering that in very ordinary moments you become an awesome generator.

That kind of silent generation of energy cannot emanate through a glamorized personality. You can be a famous personality, but a glamorized one is troubled. We refer to one who is focused on publicly but is internally dishonest. They cannot generate the energy we speak of for their fellows. Such generation is a result of looking into oneself and allowing the conditioned self to appear in its full force, in all of its tidal wave of qualities. Each of you has had occasions when your persona knocked you square on the jaw creating a sense of impending doom. To one who has discovered even a mere flickering of its own light, the dance of human conditioning becomes part of one's internal knowing. That internal knowing says, "I am being reborn into the phenomenal as I experience a collapse of my world."

A great sense of peace can come from the non-phenomenal dimension of what you are. It is not outright wonderfulness, but a very subtle, awesome knowing that all is well even as some play of difficulty passes through. You realize that you have the capacity for all experiences from the darkest to the most illumined. Resting in that capacity is resting in the non-phenomenal, non-dimensional self. And when we say non-dimensional, we include infinite dimensions of all possibilities, and also none. For, this capacity is pregnant with the recognition that nothing is happening, and within that everything is happening. This piece of the puzzle, of the paradox becomes everything because everything hinges on this non-phenomenal teaching.

Humans are most often engaged in a preferred orientation. And the number one preferred orientation is to survive. It is to eat, drink enough liquids, take care of the vehicle and be a good human with approachable conduct. So, better yourself as a human being and find new ways to apply your integrity. This is all a part of functioning as all of what you are. Doing this from the capacity of full awareness sets you up to discover anomalies in your morality and subtleties in the grey areas of your consciousness. So, how do you counteract this?

Practice hanging out in your relatedness to all beings as the search for philosophies unfolds in your intellect. Do this with an earnest intent for inquiring about your good sense. Cultivate the part of you that feels kinship with your sister and your brother and the toad. The toad is doing what it knows from its innate senses and from what it has arrived to. Your own dance is similar as you muster up your intent for integrity and enact the quality of Spirit which you are. Reflection and knowing are a part of your being. They are a gift from the universe. As you bring that on board, a transformative knowing comes into focus. It becomes practical, natural and imbibed with presence.

Do you wish to serve your brother and your sister in practical ways which demonstrate how you carry yourself as infinite love?

When you carry yourself earnestly as the very stuff of life, True Source comes through your actions. In the integrity of that source, every moment of your day can be a spiritual practice. The source of your being shows you when to be silent, when to act and how to act. Your intellect and your sense of reasoning become vehicles for that source. And from that perspective you no longer feel the impulse to out think life events, to think before things happen.

At the source of your being the genius of life is working everywhere. What is in you is also everywhere and it is one. You are a part of how life is dancing with itself and part of how life takes care of itself. And you will be taken care of even more so as you find harmony, integrity and the direct impressions of Source and its intelligence. This non-phenomenal source is the backdrop of all experiences, and your affection for it is fully allowed and established. That total openness, in turn, allows the full force of human conditioning to play through the body without resistance. Anger, sadness and fear become transformed into a great river which moves naturally. You simply allow them to be included in the overall expression of the vehicle.

In such allowing, pure source energy gets expressed in words, thoughts and actions as it plays forth. It may begin with blessing your food, or a letter, or by blessing others. So, practice utilizing your capacity to pump energy from forever into the world. The pauses and gaps between this energy's expression are evidence of the conditioned self playing. For, a residual child throwing a tantrum exists within you all. And you all have the instincts necessary for the human animal to survive and obtain food. When an infant is hungry, it cries as if its very survival depends upon getting what it needs. You do not need to be as dysfunctional as an infant. But the biological aspect of your being is built on emotional energy that might pull you in a contrary direction. As you discover your higher energy is linked directly to Source, preferred states of being will become steadier. This lesson is intended to help you reach maturity in that process.

Let all conditioning be allowed to dance completely, to be heard through all your cells and then pump through them in the higher wavelengths. Doing this emotes truth into the body. To rise, you must comprehend this greater wisdom and express it as a concept. Actualize expanded wisdom in your life. If you wish to share that with your brother and your sister you might say, "This is how I have found greater ease. This is how I have found a new way of relating with my crap. This is how I decided to see my life." When that happens, all of you become great vessels of wisdom. At no time are you expected to be more than human. In fact, you are encouraged to be human and much more.

Be humanly vulnerable, incredibly subtle to the realities of the moment and to the realities of those around you. Embrace the overall reality and its volatility. For, you are everything and it is okay to feel the pain of your brother and your sister. But, because you grasp the wisdom behind the whole play, you are meant to bring truth. When you bring truth, it lights up the room and it lights up lives sending magnificent ripples through humanity. Do not underestimate the small acts of your life, the ordinary blessings you give. If you want to feel better, find the quiet and humble parts of yourself. Give from that in small, generous ways. Give water to a thirsty person or attention to an attention starved child. Offer a piece of encouragement for the next step on someone's journey. You can say, "I have been there too. I remember when I was a child. I remember when I was hungry. I remember when I was floundering."

You all have experiences like this to relate in this school where creation unfolds. There are those who watch so many movies and experience so many victories through those movies. Many people experience revenge, anger, and being a hero as they simply watch your forms of entertainment. Of course, you could get on a plane and join up with real-life horrors experiencing them all firsthand, if that is what you want. You are here amongst humanity witnessing that kind of play. Do understand, that on this planet, you are allowed all of it. So, allow all that comes and let it come. What stays, let it stay. What goes, let it go. Think of this teaching at the beginning of the day and let it be your reference for integrity.

Within all things that come, that stay for a time, and within all the experiences in your life there is a dance. The wisdom we give speaks about becoming the groundwork, about developing a tone which sets forth a way of operating. From that base, you can be more prayerful. Your choices can feel lighter and more relaxed, like an expressive brushstroke on a fresh piece of rag-paper. You respond to what comes with natural power. Work with what comes and what remains in a posture of kindness, gentleness and integrity. Let things hang in your experience for all the time that they need. Adjust the light so it is seen more clearly as you watch with relaxed eyes and a relaxed being. Do not manage it, but do what is appropriate as it plays through.

Anchor yourself in the fact that nothing in manifest form remains forever. But the eternity that you are is forever. It is the foreverness upon which all appearance dances. You do not need to kick what is leaving in the ass. You do not need to push it to leave more quickly. You simply allow it to walk on. Of course, this is easier said than done. So, we suggest for you to have a way of relating with the whiney humans. Be honest with them and appropriate, like you would be with your own child that you love so dearly. Be with yourself in a similar way, because each of you has within an attention getting, incredibly dramatic child wreaking havoc in some way or another. It is there more than you generally recognize.

Allow for all your parts in their full appearance as their force plays through your system. You can use the empathy with this dance to emote force in your body, to pump God energy into this world.

229

Discover that which does not change and is not touched, for that is the capacity for experience. Discover that in good measure. Approach your mind-body and your energies knowing you can evoke happiness and blissful responses in life. Become more subtle, related, and natural. And while you practice that, while you heal yourself, keep one eye on the destiny of a matured aspirant. In this destiny, the human energy is allowed to play completely. It plays as part of how God stuff is more appropriately addressed in its relationship with humanity. For it is through an honest human that the purity of God can manifest.

Indeed, being an honest human is a very sophisticated, matured position. Each of you are related to all humanity through your own humanity. In this you become the mediating context of higher forces. You are part of their energies and a higher reality. Isn't this what you all desire? You might have a practical approach in your life and a useful intellect, but you also have emotion. You exist in multidimensional rooms. You are a human and a spiritual being with a soul that has many rooms of consciousness. When all of the windows are opened and the breeze is allowed to play through all of the halls and passageways, its force helps you relate to humanity. When those winds play through the dwelling that you are, they also blow through to your fellows. Your personality then comes to life. It becomes more vibrant and also gentler.

Embrace humanity and its many rooms. Hold the windows and the corridors and the many doors open. Unlock the attic and the closets. Let the winds of forever play through. For when forever washes through you, tears pour over the rocks and wash away the crud. The rocks become water, and the water becomes rock. When the water becomes rocks and the rocks become water, you will be unified with yourself as they are of the same source. Live the paradox and allow for the clarity and one pointedness to begin. You might think of yourself as a grand tree that somehow remains flexible. You are in the branches swaying easily in the wind and your whole being bends. Allow the energy we bring to saturate your branches, flow into your trunk and enliven even the woods and the soil. We bless you all in the coming days. Rhammah bids thee adieu.

STEADY

Find the steadiest place in you

When you are steady……. all of your senses are heightened and expanded

When you are steady……. the sweetness of life becomes electric

When you are steady……. colors become magnificent

When you are steady……. each soul is an equal part of a full dance

When you are steady……. you can bend, resolve, bounce back

When you are steady……. the world becomes a kaleidoscope of experience

When you are steady……. there are awesome heights of knowing

When you are steady……. you can be an ecstatic, brilliant, fire of joy

Because when you are steady there is no hunger for more than what is here
Sit quietly now and be a steady soul in your higher nature

Discourse 4: Saying Yes to the Full Spectrum of Life

In discovering the absolutely steady, the experience of the senses is heightened and expanded. You are able to hear from greater distances. When the subtlest and softest breeze touches you, your soul yields to the blessing that is the wind. Forever is felt on the skin and the whole atmosphere of the Earth is with you as that wind brushes your arm. You are with every hair on that arm and you are present with every hair on your head as it shifts with the breeze. You are with all of your senses entirely. The sweetness of this life becomes electric and the colors become magnificent as you discover that which is so steady. When you are steady there is no hunger for more than what is here.

So, focus on what is here. You earn points as you are with yourself in this magnificent way. There is a score card in your nervous system and in your brain adding up points. It notes when you get with forever as you sit with the steadiest place in you, a place where you can smell the ozone. When you enter that context, everything becomes awesomely beautiful. After enough points are earned, even a rock falling on your foot creates ecstatic intensity. For pain is intensely interesting to the steady soul. You are with every nerve that screams as they become your beloved little child and you bring love to all of it. You bring not only love of the human experience, but love of life, of each cell and its capacity to experience and rebound.

Understand this, to the steady soul it is all an equal part of a full dance. Every bit of life is poetic. And a steady soul falls for this, falls for how quiet you can be. So, quietly affirm, "Yes, it is, it simply is. I am with these senses and all that they are." Each victory with that gets put on the inner scorecard and adds up to steadiness. Steadily embrace all that is, bending and resolving, bouncing back and rebounding. You can be ever so elastic, resilient and flexible in your greater nature. When you do this, the world becomes a kaleidoscope of experiences. The eyes show you how many colors and presentations there are. Every sense expands, the sense of touch on skin, hearing in the ears, taste and all the senses at once become a knowing of this body and its connection to life. How rooted can you be in this poetry that is life? Be rooted in every gurgle in your body, every pulse, every sound that is about you. Quietly soothe every thought that runs through your head. How steady can you go?

On the whole of your planet with all of its people, how many thoughts are there? These thoughts become a spinning contraption of the multitudes. But what if they could all be seen as a distant constellation? Envision hundreds of thousands, millions and billions of thoughts hovering in space. If you can do this, you have achieved through steadiness a perception of distance. For, you can achieve distance even from the thoughts in your own head. Discover that all those thoughts are just of humanity and you are the steady, silent, ineffable quality of life. That is the steadiness I allude to. That is your destiny.

Consider your current political discussions. Every thought is flying in the air, one side and the other and there is more available than that. At first individuals may be confused until they are decidedly free of thought altogether. You might ask, "What exactly is freedom from thought altogether?" Freedom from thought means allowing all thoughts to turn, swirl, spin and just be in the soup of love. As you observe this, the steadiness which inhabits infinite love is everywhere making everything possible. It presents delusion and free will on the stage of life so that a heck of a mess, a mucky load of crap can play out in a place called humanity. This occurs in what seems to be almost forever amongst your family members, with yourself, and also with the whole of this planet. Find a place in yourself that can laugh so gleefully, laugh with it all so fully that your belly becomes an ecstatic, brilliant fire of joy.

That is the perception of a master who knows itself as the wind, the rain, the sun and the sky, the Earth and the stars. That master says yes to the blistering sun and the biting cold, to the thick air of humidity and the thin air of the mountains. In this consciousness, life is so poetic and so brilliant in its presentation. Every color is being used and your eyes will evolve to a place where you will see more color. For there is a larger spectrum of color than what you normally can see. When you are so outright steady in the "yes" of your existence, you can inhabit the full spectrum of a room in every detail. In the "yes" energy, everything becomes activated. When you are steady in your higher nature, your survival includes the awesome heights of knowing. It works like a muscle in the master, and things fall together brilliantly. This comes from the steadiness and the ability to be completely allowing.

So, sit quietly in an arena of experiences that you find pleasing. There's a whirlwind of perceptions affecting how you hear and how you interpret what you hear. Be humble about this and go to the steady place in you. Be with the subtlest of sounds in the most childlike, innocent way. Allow sound to flood in and replace the whirlwind of perception. Fall in love with sound and its textures, its colors, the way it goes into your brain and inhabits your vibration. In good faith be still, be steady and be with all of the senses. Be in yes, yes, yes! Allow this truth to reveal itself in the various sensory experiences. For all of this is miraculously put together in the soul of life. Inhabit that and work within it, allowing it to become your everyday life. To this simple teaching, say yes. Say yes!

Every cell in your body is the Beloved. When you know this truth, you are with the Beloved and It is in you. It is everywhere and everything falls apart as that reality reveals. Then, everything reforms brilliantly, for in this consciousness, ecstatic movement and a synchronicity of experiences fall in place. The world about you becomes the world of a master, because you know only that. How brilliantly you might speak if you were able to throw out all of your perceptions which have been laced together in years of complex wiring and sophistication. What if all you have done to become smart, knowledgeable and capable were thrown into the wind? You would reorganize your conceptions and the words coming from your lips would be like the wind. They would be pure knowing. All of your knowledge would finally live where it is supposed to. And you would become the Universe that simply is what it is.

You might want to say, "This intellect, has served me to this point. But the steadiest place in me has given me a profound signal. All that I have put together as fact, as function, as that which works, I now throw it to the winds. I trust reorganizing it according to the masterful way that will appear." Your words will be of the Universe in its synchronicity, its intensity, its intention and its genius. Hasn't the universe been doing things right all along? And, you are that universe. You have to sit with this teaching. And, if you sit with it, then you will have to keep sitting with it for that won't be enough. Up until now, you have been so interested in each aspect of your identity and exacting your plans for a well-done life. Instead of that you can know the soul of creation and have a robust heart. You can walk in life freely. How do you do that? You sit with this teaching, that is how.

Humans get so caught up in the notion of suffering. But what is your suffering? It is the intensity with which you are interested in your thoughts and experiences from a human point of view. You focus on that and then it just takes over. To find reality, you don't have to slap yourself, although for some it might help. You can find reality by earnestly turning toward what is. So, put your hand on your knee. Be God touching God's knee right now. And say to your mind, "This texture is of God. God is touching and sensing this texture." The capacity to detect God through your fingers may seem new to you. But you have discovered distant lands, have you not? Humans have gone to the moon, haven't they? So why not this?

There is a greater quest than those of this dimension. It is the masterful experience in all the senses, the soul of experience in all of its qualities. Acquire the steadiness that comes with that and the points earned. When you have earned these points, you can stub your toe in ecstatic intensity because the miracle of feeling has magnified. Because you are in a posture of yes, the pain exists for a shorter period of time. The cells are more resilient through the intention and presence and "yes" of a master. They heal more quickly because a master's consciousness is renewal without resistance.

So, what in your day makes you flinch? We are not asking you to stop flinching all at once. But go about quietly noticing each reaction, the resistant thoughts and earn your points. You may start to become intrigued by the idea of being an unflinching master. It will still be natural to walk away from a screeching sound, but it will not be as hellacious. In the same way that a cell can rebound, a master rebounds and goes back steadily to a quiet demeanor. A master goes to the silent place under a tree because that is so enough. Nothing more is needed. It is harmony.

To be with nature is natural to the knowing of what you are. But it should never be done with judgement. Going there as an escape in the energy of "no" will not serve you. Life will show you your attachments to "no." It will show you for as long as you need it to and for as many lifetimes as you need. You are allowed that, and nobody has to take that away from you. But in the posture of steadiness, you begin to ask why. Why keep going in a direction where there are no fruits? If you are steady in this wisdom, you will eventually understand that the most colorful fruits come from the silent resolve to be with all of life and to know the soul of it in one's own self.

You can know that the soul of a distant star is here. The souls of the many planets in your solar system are also here. It is all the soul of the distant space that begins here where you are and goes on forever expanding in this Universe. The soul of it all is right here. You do not know what it is to be a master like Rhammah, but you can, and that is a fact. I could not be here with you if that was not a fact. You would not be able to relate with these words and the soul of this truth if you were not able to find it in yourself. We are steering your rudder steadily to steadiness, right here and on course. And everything is known when you become still and embrace it all.

Many humans are attracted to new spirituality because they think it's so cool. Is there a part of you that wants others to think you are really "with it" because you study such wisdom, because you are in with the special people? Whatever of that is in you, stop it. It is a cheap trick of ego. Be so steady that you can say yes to common culture, to the sports fans in red shirts cheering their team. It is all they know and it is beautiful. It is a color under the sun, a color within humanity. Ordinary activities are just as godly as your most elevated ones. Do not in your mind be better than any of it. Say yes to all. And do not hold yourself above it because you think that you know special people, because you think you have a broader perspective. Love the most ordinary of it all. Just love it.

Human society is full of curious people. When you bring love to "Flat Land," the "Flatlanders" are everywhere. They are your neighbors. They are people next to you. They are those who found religion without finding their soul. How much love can you bring to all that? How much yes can you bring? By craving something different, you can naturally arrive in circles like this one here. You can fall into remembrance. But watch out for attraction to the magical, exotic people who wear special clothes and do special things. Stop the part of you that isn't steady, and don't fall into that "better than" trap. Steadily love whatever appears here, here in the moment. This is it.

If you really want to wake up, then you will live in this energy. This is not the same as the logic of daily life. That logic has its necessary place. But you must strive to discover what life is communicating to you. Life is showing you what is perfect for you. You are a child that is still growing up. When you are getting a slap on the wrist by life, say thank you and get over yourself. There are so many subsects of a master to be acquired. Different rays of knowing come with the soul of your being which has all of the various traits. You each have things that the other does not. Some of you have a life where you can only do humble things, nothing too spectacular. And you have to discover that you deserve to be there. You deserve it because you are the master.

There are some of you who have big energy and can create a career or discover the world. You have an easy life. You can do great things physically. You all have various gifts and they are alright, but they don't make you better than another. How can you live with all of these traits without comparing and judging? How can you stop the busy intellect which is trying to figure it all out? You can say, "For that which is steady in me, I dismiss the whirl of this thinking process. I dismiss the whirl of this mind that is grabbing for special things, special people and astounding experiences." Dismiss specialness and its attention getting qualities. Its circumstances barely serve you. You can stop and be steady. You can be with the soul of this moment. Go into the knowing of all life and disappear in it. Discover radical harmony inside and before you.

You might say, "Dear Lord of My Being, come forth. Reveal the truth that you are. I say this in faith, knowing that you will animate this life and all that it is. You will reveal yourself as everywhere. Dear Lord of My Being, show me true living. Be born in this life and see through these eyes now. I am yours and I am you Dear

Lord." Hang with that, for the Lord of Your Being is not distant. It is not somewhere far away. It may seem so because the world you live in is so tangled in a circular net of mirrors, a circular contraption of thinking. But be steady and call on the Lord of Your Being now.

When that is done, the energy of it naturally ushers forth to others. You might say, "As this breath climbs and as it falls, may all beings be blessed by the radiant power of Source energy as I abide in it, as I sit with it and affirm it. May all discover its blissful reality and its joyous nature. Dear Lord, you are appearing in every sensory experience and as the living life of this body. You are everywhere and there is only infinite love. That love is indivisibly bigger than here and there, this and that, me and you. Infinite love can surmount all of human perception. I say these words in the faith that radical transmission and radical transformation is my birthright. It is inevitable."

This sets the stage for what occurs after you've cleared a few things up in your lives. You should turn towards those who have troubles with you. Be real about them and love them. Also, love your bodies unconditionally. Love every extra pound. Look in the mirror and see forever in those eyes of yours. Look for an expression of higher understanding to come through your body. Then things will fall into place and you will lose the weight, you will look younger. When you have dropped all judgement, you get closer to yourself. You do not need to medicate your feelings because you see who you really are. And you naturally find your way to the body that works for you and with you. Your body should be in harmony with your inner self and its beauty.

That is what we mean when we say everything falls together for a master. It's okay to dibble and dabble until you get there. But we are speaking to the eventual destiny whatever time is taken. It takes whatever time it takes and that is alright. You are here now to hear about this, and to be potentially delivered to it. We've given you a strong and firm lesson tonight. Please come for more if you feel inclined to be with a challenge. Here we speak to the challenge of finding the steadiest place in you. And with that, Rhammah bids thee adieu. We are very impressed with all of you for hanging with this teaching. It is and so be it.

THANK YOU

The prize is to look into the abyss of uncertainty and say thank you

Strife is like the best opportunity and say thank you

In a breakdown, there is a silent power and say thank you

Be like the phoenix from the ashes and say thank you

Find your service within the chaotic world and say thank you

Stage it so your child says yes to the adventure because you do and say thank you

Look for the capacity to move into spiritual genius and say thank you

Discourse 5: Phoenix Rising from the Ashes

Recognizing and living in the qualities of your divinity is like discovering you are a king or a queen of a great nation. You might discover you are a sovereign, lordly reality. The truth is that all which is of this earthly realm is presented for you the observer. Discovering that is no different than the discovery of the everywhere presence of God. The truth that God is "everywhere present" allows for this personal discovery, for all that appears is of you and you are of it. To find this truth, become more reverent of life and the Source that is of that life. See each day as a divine gift from the Universe.

In the resolve to experience life as God, the mystery contacts you in such a profound way that divinity feels present in every cell and atom of your body. Your being responds with a resounding YES! It says, that lordliness is here in my heart, here in every piece of this body. It is like a hologram where one piece contains the whole. Just as any piece of intelligence in the body contains the intelligence of the whole, your spirit is a reflection of the source of life, the infinite intelligence that animates everything.

The heart of all of that, sits right where you are. Can you own that? And in the revelation of that sovereign truth, how do you become the humblest king, the most unassuming queen? For in the revelation and actualization of divinity, you know that you are simultaneously a servant to every member of your kingdom. They are of vital importance to your strength and you must care about them, tend to them and hold them in high regards. Hold in your heart the pot washer, the one who scrubs the floor, the one who participates by being a beggar playing a part in the play of your life. All lives are part of the Oneness in the great school that is this life.

This great school has a dual purpose. It creates mirrors to help you actualize what you are. It also rubs against you so that the stench of your own ego permeates your nose and enters your consciousness. Upon ripening, there is a letting go where you dissolve into the mystery. The ego surrenders to the resounding fact that there is only divinity. All that happens is of divinity. Every word that is said, every gesture that is made is all God indivisibly. That which appears before you and in you is God indivisibly, for the inseparability of spiritual truth is profoundly discovered.

Embracing this is your chance to evolve and grow as a human being. Each day you can become more willing, more capable to have skills and functions that represent what you truly are. So, respect what teaches you to think in new ways and spurs you into new skills. If you are a soul on a spiritual quest wishing for new adventures and growth as a person, then circumstances will prod you forward. Within one lifetime you will have many new adventures. Look at any human story and you will see stages of growth. Even the shifts that seems forced upon you have actually been chosen. They are chosen by the greater qualities of your spirit which is actually in charge. In the highest source or your heart of hearts, you are getting what you want.

It is confounding for you to hear this as a human. You are not sure it is true, for in calamities and problems how can you know that you are getting what you really want? Understand that there are various meanings for getting what you really want in the human dance. For example, there is the ego wanting to be the victim. It wants drama so it can stage a poor me event. It says, "See how troubled I am." Then there is, "I will be victorious," which is another way to be in a drama. Such intentions are mixed in your being with the greater impulses that seek truth and greater knowing. We urge you to get in touch with the part of you that is actually in charge. That over-soul is creating a shift so you can grow as a human, so you can grow into a more egoless awareness. Your resistance, fighting and strategizing to live as a human without too much disruption, is quite a dramatic play to watch. Many elaborate calculations are made in a day so you can have the advantage in some way.

Why not discover the higher realms of function as a joyous being? Joy is a great lubricant for function. Both you and the Universe can function a little better through your willingness to arrive as a participant in creation. Fall into step with it and following its rhythm. And how do you do this? Next time you tell your story, have a moment within the story where you say, "Thank you." Say to yourself, "I can't tell you how long I have been waiting to finally do housework." Have it feel less like, "Oh we are going to get by. We are going to handle this. I have been freed up and I don't know what I would do if I didn't have this time right now." Focus this attitude of "yes" for growth, for the victory of living in uncertainty.

You know of the victory of landing a job or landing the next check for the payment of something. Enjoy such victories, but try to animate your lives more completely. Watch your lives from a hilltop and see that they have been a process of struggle and victory. Suppose an internal objective analyst watched your lives in order to measure the progress of your higher nature. That analyst within would say, "Holy Crap! Holy Crap, I could be more grateful. I could be more resounding about the opportunity that is here in my hands. I could live more robustly for change, and watch how shift happens." Look into the abyss of uncertainty and look into all your fears of survival. The part of you in a constant grind to make everything work is being tested. Aim for some mental dialogue that can say, "I have been lost in the struggle to survive. I've been lost in petty victories. Now I have a real one to work on."

Landing a job is not a petty victory, but in comparison to higher function it is hardly a grand prize. The grand prize is to look into the abyss of uncertainty and say thank you. Know what is actualized in a heartfelt, resounding, vibrating thank you. The greatest truth is there, for humanity avoids the discovery of self most of all. Strife is the best opportunity for seeing what you are in the great mirror of life's uncertainty. It is the clearest lake where all of your fears fly into your face. You can see them so clearly as if the lake was completely still. Then say, "I am so grateful. My life has found stillness so I can see the choking in my throat and the sweating on my brow. It can help me burn through for the greatest victory possible, to know and to be free."

A silent power emerges from such an attitude. It's like the metaphor of a Phoenix rising from the ashes. Can you plunk your head into the fires that take you apart and have great faith you will become the Phoenix? As a being attached to an ego could you choose that? Perhaps not, but by saying thank you and being the fire is something you can do. It is not too much. You can prepare yourself for the victory of the greatest awakening. You can track it by thinking, "Up until this point I was struggling with uncertainties. I was fixated on little victories. Now I live in this robust 'Thank You' space while jobs come and go, while opportunities come and go, while my community and friends come and go. I found the ability to achieve a more stable and joyous quality as the dance of my kingdom plays out as it needs to."

Your span of life and all of its history goes through shifts as it finds its way. We are advanced intelligences visiting in this era, looking into opportunities for humanity. We see the volatility created by the ego and the need to see the ego for what it is so that humans can move past it into unity. Never before has it seemed so acute, how the troubles of the ego play out in humanity and create disharmony. Never before have you had the need to innovate in such a brand-new way. But the children coming up in this world right now have the capacity to innovate in radically new ways. They have the capacity to pass all of the tests put upon them.

A parent might say thank you on behalf of their child. However, some may worry about children born at this time with all of the shifts and issues going on. But this world has opportunities for those children to become strengthened in discernment. It offers the potential to use the internet in beneficial and empowering ways, rather than using it addictively. Find your path of service in this seemingly chaotic world, for you can find yourself in a universe that is unlike any other in history. Stage it so your child says yes to the adventure because you do. Enjoy the adventure of these new beings who are coming in. They are creating an attitude of yes, creating gratitude so a broader capacity for functioning exists. The finite functioning of human needs, like paying the mortgage or finding a job, will still be there. But a broader vista of understanding will expand it.

There are many layers of insight and benefit. These layers can all work together if you just have a desire to grow as a person. Be willing to grow into the spiritual reality that inhabits a profound quality. Things can just fall together for an individual who has sought a greater victory than just the material prizes. So, seek the great expanse of self-discovery and connection to the All. Comprehend your purpose with your family in spite of their slower moving neuroses. Say yes to those slow processes, for egos can be stuck for lifetimes. You all have family and the dance that goes with it. Amongst them, can you stay with your higher purpose and find your resolve? Holding true to that is not out of harmony with the rest of your dance. It is actually where the rubber hits the road.

Turn towards all those beings who irritate you, who get under your skin. Find a way to have a gratitude story. One may say, "Yes, my uncle is trouble, he is this and that, but I will get by." That version of the story has a flat quality. It's better to say, "My uncle is this or that and I have decided he is a key player in my kingdom. He is essential in the overall play for me to discover higher function and grow. He tests my ideals and my convictions. They must not be completely serving me if I feel disharmony, so he represents a part of me that doesn't yet know my connection to Source." This is a story with greater dimension. For, if you cannot look into that most troubling individual in your life, then you cannot see life. There is still some part of you hooked through aversion or attraction. When you have an aversion or attraction, you have a complex genius within trying to achieve what you want as an ego. That is not wrong, but it is just getting by.

When you embrace the greater truth, it may feel like you are flirting with disaster, but it is worth it. A disaster mindset might say, "If I say yes to my Uncle, to my Father or Mother for the sake of this 'yes' that Rhammah speaks to, I might not care about anything. I might not care that the mortgage or bills get paid. I might not care about my profession. If I don't care about how these ego attractions play in my life, I may not care about anything." There is something to such thoughts. But you will not be taken to an ultimate awakening where everything falls to the wayside before you complete the assignment to function skillfully like a master. So, look into the tests in your life that ask you to find new skills. Look for the capacity to move into the spiritual genius.

Recently we were there for the Host as he functioned peacefully and in service with a rude customer. We supported his endeavor to see this individual as he functioned from higher knowing. The challenge is that you must not look down your nose at that individual. In compassion, you realize that they are lost like you can be lost. They are lost in ego and literally lost in life. There is a gentle part of you that can work with that density. It invites you into the timing and rhythm of the Universe which dances to its own beat as come and go. You might lecture yourself saying, "I work in a highly functioning way when I am less fettered. I can play the game in a masterful way, adjusting various areas in my life as if everything is right. I trust life and everything is in perfect function."

Envision your house as a matrix of energy. Send a signal into humanity. "Here I am, joyously present for all. And because I have joy and gratitude, this capacity to function has reached new heights. I'm not contracted so I can think. My occupation of choice has collapsed, but I maintain a steadiness. I can share what's left and move forward, capturing more opportunities than ever before." That is functioning as a master. You are a dream character with a masterful overlay. And when you act masterfully, life as it is will fit like an exquisitely designed glove. What would it be like to function so peacefully, so powerfully in all the turns of one's life? Practice a bit at a time to hold this space.

All of forever, the highest of heavens lives right here. Is that something you achieve or is it a reality you insist on because it is true? Sit with that and own what is happening from a kingly space. When a king breathes, that is the breath of a kingdom. Your breath is the breath of the Universe. Your body is connected to all of life. It is interrelated with all realities. Make even the smallest advance in holding this consciousness and devote it to lifting the universe. You can say, "As I inhabit this breath may all beings be lifted by a loving healing power. With this very breath may every atom in this universe be lifted by this radiant reality which is Godly awareness." That is the resonance of actualizing. Everything you do counts, so have reverence for your every action. What you do in each moment lifts the All. That is what it is like to live in an "avatar" state of being.

Practicing this is selfless service in the highest way possible, and through it you will discover sovereign humility. Your sovereignty is in reverence for life and giving yourselves over, surrendering to the Source of Life. Discover your connection and a genius that is supplied by the Source will arise. In the discovery of your non-separateness from that Source, you will know Source, walking its walk and living in its stride. With life in charge of itself, you discover your highest will within it. This is a practice you get better at with practice. But know that you can be the avatar right now. The highest heaven plays through you and lifts your friends and family. And in that context, it is easier to look at your crap. You might say, "This part of me, the crap part of my function, is south of my lordly truth. I believe in you, my very self. I know the god within is orchestrating everything perfectly."

Is such thinking true for you? If it's not, how do you make it so? A very direct way to do that is to say thank you. "Thank you for this test, this opportunity to grow and see what is in the way of my unity and connection with all." Hold your enemy so close in your mind that you transform. Become rearranged by this position. This is absolutely the magic pill. Can you swallow it? A person who has robbed you in the worst way, hold them in mind. Speak to life, to the genius that is at work and say thank you. By doing this you are unhooking yourself from a mediocre way of functioning and moving into a masterful way of functioning.

That is a capacity that is in all of you. In this posture, you are present with your body, saying yes to the body in contrast to all the ways humanity says no to their bodies. You are the cutting edge, living in that loving vibration. Move out of judgment, out of heavy criticism, out of self-consciousness and shame towards your body. For you are moving out of "I am body" and moving into "I am one with All." Why get lost in humanity's fixations when you can be kind to your brother, to your sister and to yourself. Wake up asking yourself what your song is, for you can sing your song on this day. Today I can sing a song, get over something, reach into a poetic quality in my being and create something brilliant out of the ashes.

Can you get excited about that? Inspire yourself and inspire others. Embrace and appreciate even the heaviest aspects of self and life. Appreciate the higher potentials and know that in all the layers of yourself there is no issue. You are whole. Pray, "Dear Lord of Life, I know in the journey of surrender I discover you as my very own self. I discover your will as my highest expression. Dear Lord that is in me, I call on you now to inhabit this breath, to inhabit this gesture. I am prayerfully in the indivisible space where all worlds meet. I am aligned reverently in Oneness, and by doing this I lift humanity. Being with it in gratitude, I lift the All."

When you lift yourself in this most dedicated and radiant way, the many worlds are different. Forever and eternity are different. Be masters owning your position in the Universe. The great king is the humblest being. The wretched king is not. As you become used to taking little steps, they get bigger because their meaning becomes clearer. In the hero's story, little steps towards resolution may seem small until they come into focus in your consciousness and become your life. Pay attention to the new adventure that is upon you. Pay attention to how quiet that new beginning is. Sensitize yourself to that and be less taken by the grand things. Focus on the subtle shifts in your life that cumulate and become your ability to function brilliantly.

You can start with finding a way to be with a subtle aspect of your being, like how your eyes blink, how your chest rises. Then repeat, "With each rise of this chest as the breath moves, may all beings be blessed by this radiant presence." By actualizing this simple truth, all beings are blessed. That is the greatest uphill movement. It is so simple. Know that I am with you as you transfigure into the great player in your lives and a great player in other's lives as well. I am with you as you are the dish washer or the one who scrubs the floor. No task is menial, for you are of all these grand things and more. Everything matters and I acknowledge you all as my very own self. I am in service to you all. And with that Rhammah bids thee adieu. You are all doing grandly, indeed.

WHY NOT.

GROUP DISCUSSION QUESTIONS can be found at: www.rhammah.com

www.ingramcontent.com/pod-product-compliance
Lightning Source LLC
Chambersburg PA
CBHW051817090426
42736CB00011B/1520